WEIMAR and NAZI GERMANY

Stephen Lee

Heinemann Educational Publishers
Halley Court, Jordan Hill, Oxford OX2 8EJ
a division of Reed Educational and Professional
Publishing Ltd

OXFORD MADRID ATHENS FLORENCE PRAGUE
CHICAGO PORTSMOUTH NH (USA) MEXICO CITY
SAO PAULO SINGAPORE KUALA LUMPUR TOKYO
MELBOURNE AUCKLAND IBADAN NAIROBI
KAMPALA GABORONE JOHANNESBURG

First published 1996

99 98 97 96
10 9 8 7 6 5 4 3 2 1

British Library Cataloguing in Publication Data
is available from the British Library on request.

ISBN 0 435 30920 X

Produced by Visual Image, Street, Somerset
Illustrations by Visual Image
Printed by Mateu Cromo in Spain
Cover design by The Wooden Ark Studio
Cover photo of a 1934 German Youth Movement poster,
reproduced courtesy of the Imperial War Museum.

The publishers would like to thank Dr Stephen Vickers and David Aldred for their comments on the original manuscript.

This book is for Charlotte

Acknowledgements
The publishers would like to thank the following for permission to reproduce photographs:

Akademie der Kunste: 36; AKG London: 9 top, 11E, 15, 18, 31, 32, 47, 62, 65, 71, 84; Bauhaus Archive: 16B; Bildarchiv Preussischer Kulturbesitz: 16A, 17B; Bilderdienst Suddeutscher Verlag: 4, 5, 14, 26, 35, 40, 42 right, 51, 53D, 73, 81G, 86 top; Bridgeman Art Library: 57C, D and E; Bundesarchiv Koblenz: cover, 13J, 66J; Centre for the Study of Cartoon and Caricature, Univ. of Kent, David Low/Solo Syndication: 42D; Lujcan Dobroszycki: 87; Zoe Dominic: 17D; The Federal Republic of Germany: 57B; The C.L. Hall Collection: 13I, 23, 25, 45, 46, 58I, 61, 67, 76E, 76F; The Heartfield Archive: 20; Chris Honeywell: 11D; The Hoover Institution Archives: 21, 35H; Hulton Getty Collection: 41, 43 left, 62, 78, 92; Imperial War Museum: 77D, 81E; Kunstbibliotek Berlin: 66K; Kunstmuseum Berne: 56; Pictorial Press: 81G; Popperfoto: 9 bottom, 42G, 82; Topham Picture Source: 39, Ullstein Bilderdienst: 7, 9, 13H, 48, 53E, 68, 86 bottom, 93; Weimar Picture Library: 33, 52; Wiener Library: 34, 44, 50, 54, 55, 58H; Yad Vashem Holocaust Martyrs' and Heroes' Remembrance Authority: 88C and D

Details of written sources
In some sources the wording or sentence structure has been simplified to ensure that the source is accessible.

Richard Bessel (ed.), *Life in the Third Reich*, Oxford University Press, 1987: 4.2M
M. Berwick, *The Third Reich*, Wayland, 1971: 5.6A, 5.6B
Christabel Bielenberg, *The Past is Myself*, Corgi, 1970: 5.7.1
E. Amy Buller, *Darkness over Germany*, Longman, 1945: 4.3H
H.C. Brandenburg, *Die Geschichte der Hitlerjugend*, Cologne, 1968: 2.6.1
M. Broszat, *The Hitler State*, London, 1981: 5.3B
Karl von Clausewitz, *On War*, Penguin, 1982: 5.1A
The Daily Telegraph, May 1933: 4.6.4
S.C. Dekel and L.M. Lagnado, *Children of the Flames*, London, 1991: 5.3E
Lucjan Dobroszycki (ed.), *The Chonicle of the Lodz Ghetto 1941 – 1944*, Yale University Press, 1994: 5.4A
Bernt Engelmann, *In Hitler's Germany*, Mandarin, 1989: 4.6.2
Anne Frank, *The Diary of Anne Frank*, Pan Books, 1968: 5.3G
Sara Grober, *Jewish Public Activities in the Lodz Ghetto*, 1979: 5.4B
R. Grunberger, *A Social History of the Third Reich*, Weidenfeld and Nicolson, 1971: 4.1F, 4.3D, 4.3E, 4.3F
C.W. Guillebaud, *The Economic Recovery of Germany from 1933 to the incorporatioin of Austria in March 1938*, Macmillan, 1939: 4.1A
S. William Halperin, *Germany Tried Democracy*, New York, 1965: 1.5B
S.M. Harrison, *World Conflict in the Twentieth Century*, Macmillan, 1987:
K. Hildebrand, *The Third Reich*, London, 1984: 5.3A
Adolf Hitler, *Mein Kampf*, (1924 trans. R. Mannheim) Sentry Paperbacks, 1943: 1.9.1, 2.2G, 3.3A, 3.8.3, 5.1C, 5.1D
Adolf Hitler, *Second Book*, New York, 1962: 2.2H, 5.1E
Illustrated London News, August 1936: 3.8.5
Ian Kershaw, *History Today*, 'The Hitler Myth', Nov. 1985: 4.5B
A. Klonne, *Youth in the Third Reich*, 1982: 4.2I
H. Krausnick, *The Anatomy of the SS State*, London, 1968: 3.3G
J. Laver (ed.), *Imperial and Weimar Germany*, Hodder and Stoughton, 1992: 1.8C, 2.2F, 2.4B, 2.4E, 2.4G, 3.5B, 4.2D, 5.5A, 5.5C
G. Le Bon, *The Crowd: A Study of the Popular Mind*, Ernest Benn, 1952: 2.6.5
R. Leonhard, *A Fairy Tale of Christmas*, (trans. J. Cleugh): 1.8A
W. Maser, *Hitler's Letters and Notes*, Heinemann, 1974: 5.6C
G. Mosse, *Nazi Culture*, W.H. Allen, 1966: 4.2H
J. Noakes, *History Today*, 'Social Outcasts in Nazi Germany', Dec. 1985: 4.4A
J. Noakes and G. Pridham (eds.) *Documents on Nazism 1919 – 1945*, Jonathan Cape, 1974: 2.1B, 2.1C, 2.1D, 2.1F, 2.1G, 2.2C, 2.3A, 2.3B, 2.3D, 2.3E, 3.3J, 3.4B, 3.4H, 3.5G, 3.8, 4.1I, 4.3B, 5.2F, 5.3C, 5.3H, 5.5B, 5.6E
J. Remak, *The Nazi Years*, Prentice-Hall, 1969: 2.2B, 2.2D, 2.4D, 3.2C, 3.2E, 3.3H, 3.3I, 3.4C, 3.4E, 3.5E, 3.5H, 4.5A, 5.1B, 5.2C, 5.3F
Martin Roberts, *Britain and Europe, 1848 – 1980*, Longman, 1986: 5.7.2
Philip Sauvain, *The Era of the Second World War*, Stanley Thornes, 1993: 5.7.4
William Shirer, *Rise and Fall of the Third Reich*, Pan Books, 1968: 2.6.3
L.L. Snyder, *The Weimar Republic*, Van Nostrand, 1966: 1.2B, 1.2D, 1.3A, 1.5G, 1.6B, 1.6D
Otto Strasser, *Hitler and I*, London, 1940: 2.6.4
Sir J. Wheeler-Bennett, *The Nemesis of Power*, Macmillan, 1953: 3.2F
Schools Council General Studies Project, *Nazi Education*, Longman, 1972: 4.2B
The Times, 4 October 1929: 1.9.2
The United States Strategic Bombing Survey, Overall Report, Washington, 1945: 5.4H

CONTENTS

CHAPTER 1 THE BIRTH, STRUGGLE AND DEATH OF THE WEIMAR REPUBLIC 1919–33

1.1 How did the Weimar Republic get its name? 4
1.2 How did Germany become a Republic? 4
1.3 How democratic was the Weimar Republic? 6
1.4 Who supported and who opposed the Weimar Republic? 8
1.5 Why did the Republic face a crisis 1919–23? 10
1.6 Recovery (1): The Stresemann era 1923–9 14
1.7 Recovery (2): Art and culture 16
1.8 Why did crisis return to the Republic 1929–33? 18
1.9 Exercise 22

CHAPTER 2 THE RISE OF HITLER TO 1933

2.1 How did Hitler come to dominate the Nazi Party? 23
2.2 What were Hitler's main ideas? 27
2.3 How did Hitler change his strategy 1925–9? 30
2.4 How did Hitler seize his opportunity 1929–33? 32
2.5 Hitler's rise to power: a summary 37
2.6 Exercise 39

CHAPTER 3 THE NAZI RÉGIME 1933–45

3.1 What was the Nazi revolution? 40
3.2 The 'legal' revolution 40
3.3 How did the Nazis enforce their political power? 43
3.4 What opposition was there to Nazi policies? 48
3.5 How did the Nazis build the racial state? 52
3.6 How did the Nazis rebuild German culture? 56
3.7 How did Hitler change the German economy? 60
3.8 Exercise 62

CHAPTER 4 LIFE IN THE THIRD REICH

4.1 Did the people benefit from Nazi economic policies? 63
4.2 What was it like to be young in Nazi Germany? 67
4.3 How did life change for women and the family? 71
4.4 What was it like to be a minority group in Nazi Germany? 74
4.5 What did the German people think of Hitler? 75
4.6 Exercise 78

CHAPTER 5 THE IMPACT OF WAR ON THE THIRD REICH

5.1 Hitler's attitude to war 79
5.2 How did the people adjust to the experience of war? 80
5.3 War and the Holocaust 83
5.4 Life in the Ghetto of Lodz 87
5.5 Resistance to Hitler during the War 89
5.6 The end of the Third Reich 91
5.7 Exercise 93

GLOSSARY 94

INDEX 95

THE BIRTH, STRUGGLE AND DEATH OF THE WEIMAR REPUBLIC 1919–33

1.1 How did the Weimar Republic get its name?

Weimar is a town of striking beauty in the German state of Saxony. It was one of Europe's great cultural centres, in which many artists, poets and composers had lived and worked over the centuries.

A hundred and fifty miles to its north-east is Berlin, a vast city within the state of Prussia. When Prussia united the other states with itself in 1871, Berlin became the capital of a new German Empire, or *Reich*, which gloried in being Europe's greatest military power.

In 1918 this Empire lay in ruins and, as we shall see, there was violence in Berlin. For a few months, early in 1919, Weimar became the temporary capital before this was switched back to Berlin. This new German **republic** kept the name Weimar throughout its brief history as a reminder of the more cultured and less aggressive side of the German nation.

Source A

▲ **Philipp Scheidemann proclaiming Germany a republic, 9 November 1918.**

1.2 How did Germany become a republic?

The Weimar Republic was born out of Germany's defeat in the First World War (1914–18). The German armies had failed to break through the western front against Britain and France. The German people had also suffered hardship and starvation as a result of a blockade of their ports by the British navy. By October 1918 the situation had become so bad that sailors mutinied in Kiel and Hamburg, while soldiers refused to obey orders in Cologne. On 9 November the **Kaiser**, or Emperor, abdicated and fled to the Netherlands. Out of this chaos of the collapsing Reich, a new government somehow had to be formed.

Source B

Long and incessant toil is before us. Nothing must be done which brings dishonour to the labour movement. Stand united and loyal and be conscious of your duty. The old and rotten – the monarchy has broken down. Long live the new! Long live the German Republic!

▶ **The conclusion of Scheidemann's speech proclaiming Germany a republic, 9 November 1918.**

There were two main possibilities. One was the formation of a democracy on the lines of France or the United States of America (USA). On 9 November Philipp Scheidemann, who was one of the leaders of the Social Democrats (the largest political party in Germany), proclaimed Germany a democratic republic on the balcony of the ***Reichstag*** (parliament building).

Another possibility was that Germany would become a communist state similar to Russia under Lenin. This was the ambition of the **Spartacus League** led by Rosa Luxemburg and Karl Liebknecht.

In January 1919 the Spartacists tried to seize power with an armed uprising in Berlin. The Social Democrats, under Scheidemann and Friedrich Ebert, saw the Spartacists as a great danger. Ebert did a deal with General Groener allowing the army to put down the Spartacists as long as the Social Democrats were left alone. Groener had a great deal of influence within the army and wanted Germany to have a democratic government. Thousands of Spartacists were killed in the bloodbath which followed in Berlin, and Rosa Luxemburg and Karl Liebknecht were both shot in cold blood. The Communists never forgot this and, throughout the history of the Republic, they saw the Social Democrats as their deadliest enemies. This was later to be of vital importance.

ROSA LUXEMBURG (1871–1919)

Rosa Luxemburg was born in Poland [then a province of Russia], but became a German citizen as a result of her marriage. She joined the Social Democrats but was imprisoned in 1915 for opposing the First World War. She helped found the Spartacus League, which was transformed into the German Communist Party [KPD]. She was nicknamed 'Red Rosa' and was a good speaker and impressive writer. She and Karl Liebknecht were killed by the army in the uprising in Berlin in January 1919.

QUESTIONS

1 Examine Sources B and D. What do they have in common and in what ways do they differ?

2 Examine Sources A and C. What do they have in common and in what ways do they differ?

3 'Scheidemann and the Social Democrats were moderate but the Spartacists were extreme'. Do the text and sources support this statement? Explain your answer.

Source C

▲ **A Spartacist meeting in Berlin, 30 December 1918.**

Source D

PROLETARIANS! MEN AND WOMEN OF LABOUR! COMRADES!

The revolution has made its entry into Germany. The masses of soldiers, who for four years were driven to the slaughterhouse for the sake of the capitalists' profits, the masses of workers, who for four years were exploited, crushed, and starved, have revolted. The Kaiser and the Crown Prince have fled from the country. Workers' and Soldiers' Councils have been formed everywhere. We call to you: 'Arise for the the struggle! Arise for action!'

▲ **An extract from the *Spartacist Manifesto*, 29 November 1918.**

1.3 How democratic was the Weimar Republic?

Source A

Article 1: The German Reich is a Republic. Political authority comes from the people.
Article 22: The delegates [in the Reichstag] are elected by universal, equal, direct and secret suffrage by men and women over twenty years of age, according to proportional representation.
Article 48: In the event that the public order and security are seriously disturbed or endangered, the Reich President may take the measures necessary for their restoration, intervening, if necessary, with the aid of the armed forces.
Article 54: The Chancellor and the Ministers require for the exercise of their office the confidence of the Reichstag.

▲ **Extracts from the Constitution of the Weimar Republic.**

The new Reichstag, or parliament, first met in Weimar early in 1919 because of the disturbances in Berlin, but it then moved back to the permanent capital. Extracts from the **Constitution** of the Weimar Republic are shown in Source A.

In some ways the Constitution set up one of the most advanced **democracies** in Europe. Men and women were given the vote at 20. This compared with a voting age in Britain of 21 for men and 30 for some women. The number of seats for each party in the Reichstag was to be based on the total number of votes won by that party: this is known as **proportional representation**. The head of the government, or Chancellor, had to have the support of a majority in the Reichstag. Finally, Germany was a **federation** – each state, such as Bavaria and Prussia, had its own state government.

On the other hand, there were some ways in which democracy might be limited. The head of state, or President, had the power to appoint and dismiss the Chancellor. If he considered that there was an emergency he could use Article 48 to suspend democracy for a time and rule by decree (laws which he would impose). In addition, the second chamber of parliament, the Reichsrat, had members appointed by the state governments, and one of these states, Prussia, had an overall majority in it.

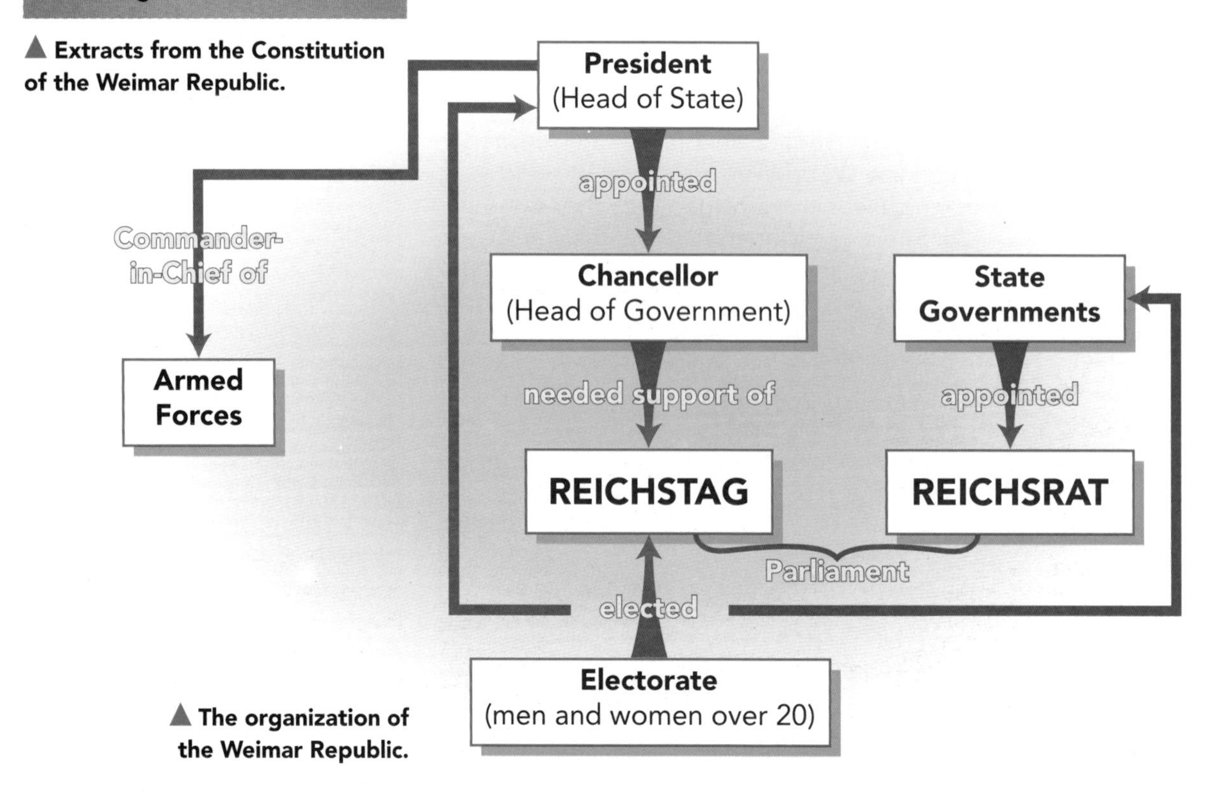

▲ **The organization of the Weimar Republic.**

Coalition governments

These rules were actually intended to balance each other. Democracy would work most of the time; but there were special powers to protect it against sudden violence and chaos. Unfortunately, the Constitution was to hit a series of problems over the next fourteen years. Because of proportional representation no party ever had an overall majority in the Reichstag. This meant that all governments were **coalitions** which had to be put together from several parties. This was possible in good times, but during a crisis it would prove impossible and make it tempting for the President to avoid democracy altogether and rule by decree. This is what happened after 1930.

The army, civil servants and judges

To make the Republic even more unstable, there were several groups which were very conservative and traditional. They preferred the way that Germany was run before 1918, when the Kaiser was the head of state. One of these groups was the army. Although it had been defeated in the First World War, it was re-formed as the **Reichswehr** and its commanding officers, such as Hindenburg, Ludendorff and von Bardeleben disliked democracy. Another group was the **civil service**, which slowed down some of the reforms attempted by the Weimar government. A third was the **judiciary**, or the judges and the law courts. They were more sympathetic to the groups of the extreme right than to those of the left.

Thus, the Weimar Republic was a new democracy which was built upon old conservative foundations. Along with the problems in the Constitution, this did not make for a promising future.

Source C

▲ **A cartoon showing how judges were reluctant to deal severely with right-wing activists.**

QUESTIONS

1 Were the following strengths or weaknesses in the Weimar Constitution:
  a Proportional representation
  b Article 48?
  Explain your answer.

2 a Why were some groups unenthusiastic about democracy?
  b How did this affect the Weimar government?

3 Using the text and sources was the Weimar Republic an 'advanced' democracy? Explain your view.

Source B

◀ **The Reichswehr came under the command of officers who had fought in the First World War. On the left is Ludendorff, in the forefront is von Bardeleben. They are wearing the uniforms and helmets of the old Second Reich.**

1.4 Who supported and who opposed the Weimar Republic?

From 1919 onwards, there were many different political parties. These ranged from the extreme left to the extreme right, with the more moderate in-between.

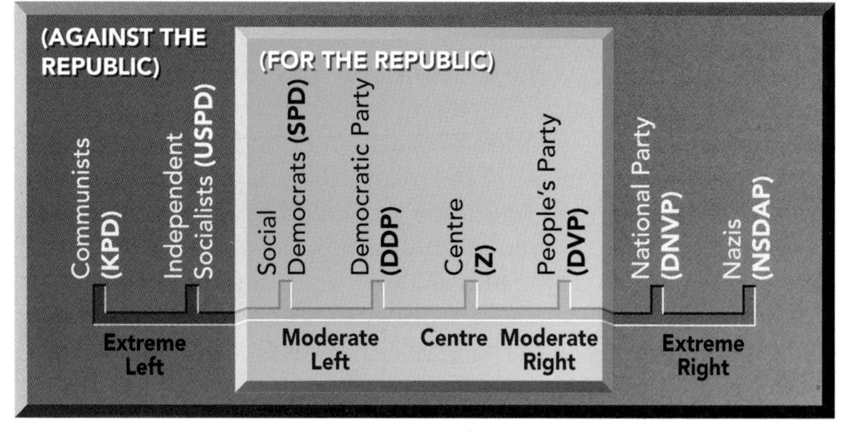

▲ **The parties of the Weimar Republic, ranging from left-wing to right-wing. (They are given English names but German initials.)**

Which political parties supported Weimar?

At the far left were two parties: the Spartacists (who soon became known as the **German Communist Party**, or **KPD**) and the **Independent Socialists** (**USPD**). They joined together and demanded a workers' state like the one in **Bolshevik** Russia. The communists hated the Weimar Republic, because it was a western democracy and it had put down the Spartacist uprising in 1919.

Then came a series of more moderate parties. The **Social Democratic Party** (**SPD**) set up the Republic and its leaders, Ebert and Scheidemann, became the first President and Chancellor. The SPD believed in a democratic system, but it was strongly opposed to communism. The **Democratic Party** (**DDP**) was formed by lawyers and intellectuals, including Hugo Preuss, the author of the Constitution. The **Centre Party** (**Z**) was made up of Catholics from all the social classes. It was more cautious about reform than the DDP and SPD, but much preferred these parties to the extremes of either side. To their right was the **People's Party** (**DVP**). It was concerned about Germany's national reputation but still supported the Republic; in fact its leader, Gustav Stresemann, was to become the Republic's greatest politician.

		Jan 1919	June 1920	May 1924	Dec 1924	May 1928	Sept 1930	July 1932	Nov 1932
(AGAINST THE REPUBLIC)	Nazis (NSDAP)	–	–	32	14	12	107	230	196
(AGAINST THE REPUBLIC)	National Party (DNVP)	44	71	95	103	73	41	37	52
(FOR THE REPUBLIC)	People's Party (DVP)	19	65	45	51	45	30	7	11
(FOR THE REPUBLIC)	Centre (Z)	91	64	65	69	62	68	75	70
(FOR THE REPUBLIC)	Democratic Party (DDP)	75	39	28	32	25	20	4	2
(FOR THE REPUBLIC)	Social Democrats (SPD)	165	102	100	131	153	143	133	121
(AGAINST THE REPUBLIC)	Independent Socialists (USPD)	22	84	–	–	–	–	–	–
(AGAINST THE REPUBLIC)	Communists (KPD)	–	4	62	45	54	77	89	100

▲ **The results of national elections to the Reichstag, 1919–32.**

Finally, on the extreme right were two parties which hated the Republic. The **National Party** (**DNVP**) was anti-democratic and wanted a system based more on authority. It also wanted to see the revival of Germany as a military power. The **German Workers' Party** (**DAP**) was soon to become the **National Socialist German Workers' Party** (**NSDAP**) or Nazi Party, under Adolf Hitler. In 1919 it was unimportant: its time came later.

DATE	PARTY OF CHANCELLOR	CHANCELLOR	PRESIDENT
1919	SPD	Scheidemann	Ebert (SPD)
1919–20	SPD	Bauer	
1920	SPD	Müller	
1920–1	Z	Fehrenbach	
1921–2	Z	Wirth	
1922–3	Non-party	Cuno	
1923	DVP	Stresemann	
1923–5	Z	Marx	
1925–6	Non-party	Luther	Hindenburg (Non-party)
1926–8	Z	Marx	
1928–30	SPD	Müller	
1930–2	Z	Brüning	
1932	Non-party	Papen	
1932	Non-party	Schleicher	
1933	Nazi	Hitler	

◀ **The governments of the Republic 1919–33, showing the parties involved, the Chancellors and the Presidents.**

Who supported the parties?

The use of the secret ballot means that it is difficult to say precisely which people supported which parties. But it is possible to make a number of general statements.

Most of the working class would have voted for the parties of the left. Whether they supported the KPD or SPD would have depended on whether they thought that the Republic offered them any prospects. Most preferred the SPD.

The middle class varied widely. Some preferred the ideas of the DDP, some felt that the DVP would provide more emphasis on national recovery, some again were suspicious of the Republic and voted for the DNVP. Later, the middle class was to provide much of the support for the Nazis. Wealthy industrialists and businessmen were most likely to vote for the DNVP. Finally, the Centre Party (Z) was most interested in preserving the interests of religion. Hence it was supported by those, especially Catholics, who put religion first – whatever their class.

At first the moderate parties did very well in national elections. But, gradually, the extreme parties became more and more important. The reason for these developments will be described over the next eleven pages.

QUESTIONS

1 Make out a chart like the one below. Fill in the details using the information on page 8.

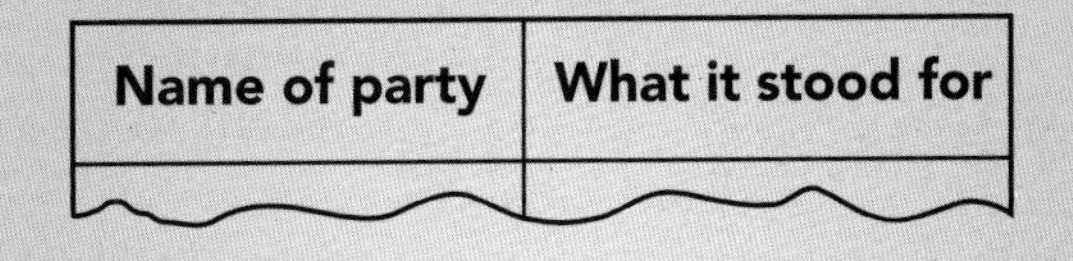

2 Study the election results for 1919–32 (page 8).

a Draw a graph using an outline like the one below.

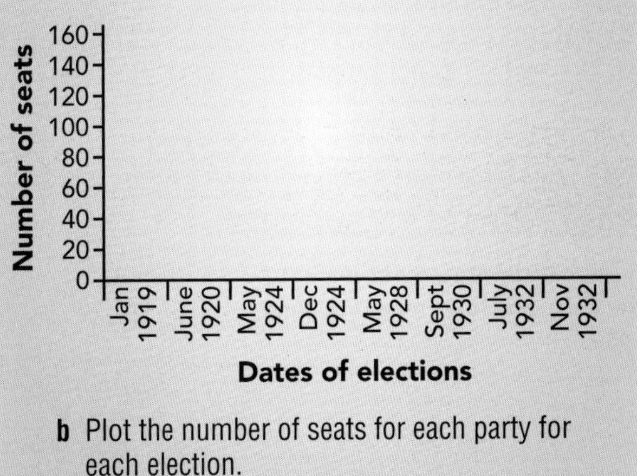

b Plot the number of seats for each party for each election.

c What voting trends does your graph show?

3 Study the table showing the governments of the Republic (page 9). What was the main disadvantage of coalition government?

A 'crisis' is strictly the point in a disease where the patient is finely balanced between recovery on one side and death on the other. The Weimar Republic experienced two periods of crisis. The first was between 1919 and 1923, from which it recovered. The second, between 1929 and 1933, killed it.

The crisis of 1919–23 had three causes. One was external: the treatment of Germany by the Allies. The others were internal: economic collapse and political *putsches* (or revolts). All three were interconnected.

Source A

The Allied Governments affirm, and Germany accepts, the responsibility of Germany and her allies for causing all the losses and damage to which the Allied Governments and peoples have been subjected as a result of the War.

▲ **Article 231 (the 'War Guilt' clause) from the Treaty of Versailles.**

Source B

Yielding to overpowering might, the government of the German Republic declares itself ready to accept and sign the peace treaty. But in so doing, the government of the German Republic in no way abandons its conviction that these conditions of peace are unjust.

▲ **An official statement made by the German Government in June 1919.**

Germany and the Treaty of Versailles

Germany had surrendered to the Allies on 11 November 1918, two days after the formation of the Republic. In June 1919 the terms of the Treaty of Versailles were announced. Germany was held to be 'guilty' of causing the First World War and all the damage resulting from it. Hence, the German nation was expected to provide compensation.

Germany also lost a large amount of territory. Alsace and Lorraine were given to France; Eupen and Malmédy to Belgium; and Posen and West Prussia to Poland. Other areas were given up after the population had given their consent in **plebiscites**, or popular votes. As a result Northern Schleswig went to Denmark and Upper Silesia to Poland.

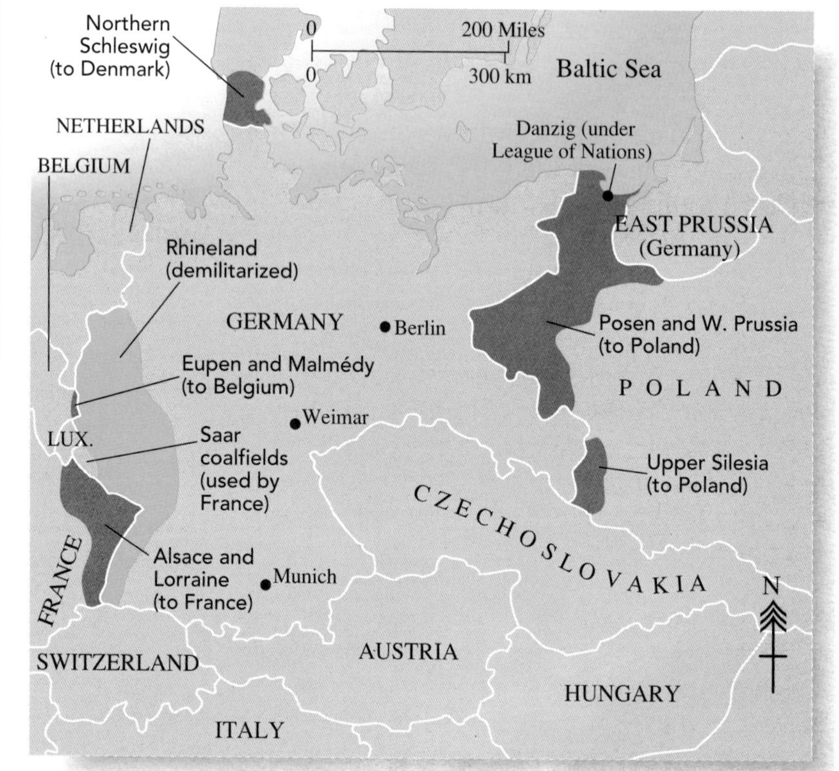

▶ **Germany's territorial losses by the Treaty of Versailles, 1919.**

All of Germany's overseas colonies were given to the victors, especially Britain and France, as **mandates**, or territories held in trust until they were ready for independence.

Germany was also cut back severely as a military power. It was allowed a navy of only six battleships, an army of no more than 100,000 volunteers and no airforce at all. The Rhineland was **demilitarized** to protect France. Finally, Germany had to pay the costs of the war. Many of its railway engines and rolling stock were confiscated and, in 1921, it was announced that it should pay £6,600 million in **reparations**.

The German people found these terms extremely difficult to accept. The Government complained that it had no choice, but the popular press called for revenge – at first against the Allies, but later against the Government which had signed the Treaty. The Government found itself in an impossible position and the crisis was to deepen.

Source C

Vengeance! German nation! Today in the Hall of Mirrors the disgraceful treaty is being signed. Do not forget it. The German people will with unceasing labour press forward to renconquer the place among nations to which it is entitled. Then will come vengeance for the shame of 1919.

▲ **An extract from *Deutsche Zeitung*, a German newspaper, 28 June 1919.**

The growth of inflation

After 1921 the German economy experienced **hyper-inflation**, triggered largely by the Allies' announcement of the reparations bill. Another cause was that wealthy businessmen speculated with the currency, or tried to make a quick profit.

Source D

▲ **Original German banknotes from 1921 and 1923 in denominations of millions of marks.**

Source E

◀ **German children playing with bundles of banknotes made worthless by the hyper-inflation, 1923.**

The value of the mark declined rapidly between 1921 and 1923. In January 1923 French troops invaded the **Ruhr** to collect reparations still owing to them. This brought about the complete collapse of the currency. The mark became worthless and many people lost their life savings or pensions.

This created a dangerous situation for the future. Although Germany recovered in 1923, as we shall see, many Germans found the economic crisis after 1929 all the more difficult to bear because it was the second time around. In 1924 the middle classes were prepared to give the Republic another chance – but not in 1930, when more and more people abandoned the parties they had once supported.

Source F

1918
0.63 marks

1922
163 marks

Jan. 1923
250 marks

July 1923
3,465 marks

Sept. 1923
1,512,000 marks

Nov. 1923
201,000,000,000 marks

▲ **The rising cost of a loaf of bread in Berlin.**

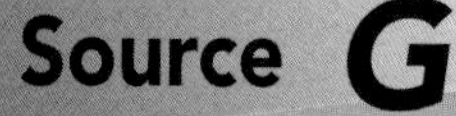

As soon as I received my salary I rushed out to buy the daily necessities. My daily salary, as editor of the periodical *Soziale Praxix*, was just enough to buy one loaf of bread and a small piece of cheese or some oatmeal . . . An acquaintance of mine, a clergyman, came to Berlin from a suburb with his monthly salary to buy a pair of shoes for his baby; he could buy only a cup of coffee.

▲ **Dr Frieda Wunderlich, a journalist, describes the effects of hyper-inflation, 1923.**

What did the Government do to prevent the crisis of 1923? The answer is very little; in fact it fuelled inflation by authorizing the printing of masses of paper notes by 300 paper mills and 2,000 printing shops. The Allies considered that this was a deliberate attempt to avoid paying reparations – and certainly the German Government had little incentive to strengthen the economy so that regular payments could resume. It was, however, playing a dangerous game, for there were those who saw economic collapse as a perfect opportunity to try to destroy the Republic.

Two attempts to overthrow the Republic

In March 1920 **Dr Wolfgang Kapp** marched on Berlin with 5,000 supporters intending to set up a right-wing government. The flag of Imperial Germany (the old Second Reich) was raised in Berlin by some of his supporters (Source H). The Government withdrew to Dresden and called for a general strike of German workers in the essential services: gas, water, electricity and transport. Without these, Kapp could not hope to govern, and so gave up and fled abroad.

Another attempt was made in November 1923, at the height of the economic crisis. **Adolf Hitler**, who had recently taken over the leadership of the Nazi Party, felt that the Government was ripe for destruction. He and General Ludendorff therefore tried to organize a march from Munich to Berlin (Source I). The march was broken up by Bavarian police in Munich itself, and Hitler was arrested. A fuller account of the Munich *Putsch* is given in Chapter 2.

Both these uprisings were attempted by the right wing. Kapp's looked back to the old Germany, or Second Reich, while Hitler's looked forward to a new Germany, or **Third Reich**. In this respect they were very different. But they shared one thing: both blamed the Republic for the surrender of Germany and the Treaty of Versailles.

Source H

▲ **The flag of the old Second Reich being raised in Berlin during the Kapp *Putsch*, March 1920.**

Source I

▲ **The swastika flag of the Nazi Party being shown during the Munich *Putsch*, 1923.**

Both Kapp and Hitler spread the false accusation that the German army had been 'stabbed in the back' by German politicians. By this they meant that the Government had surrendered while the army was still willing to fight. The right did not succeed in destroying the Republic with this lie in the early 1920s. Ten years later, however, the 'stab in the back' argument was to be used again, this time with greater success.

Source J

▶ **A poster accusing the German Government of 'stabbing the army in the back' in 1918.**

QUESTIONS

1. In what ways are Sources B and C **a** similar and **b** different? How would you explain these similarities and differences?
2. Study the text and Sources H and I. In what ways were the Kapp *Putsch* (1920) and the Munich *Putsch* (1923) **a** similar and **b** different?
3. Which of the following was the most serious problem for the Republic:
   a The Treaty of Versailles
   b Inflation
   c The Kapp *Putsch*, 1920
   d The Munich *Putsch*, 1923?
4. Why would the right-wing supporters of Kapp and Hitler have agreed with Source J?

1.6 Recovery (1): The Stresemann era 1923–9

The crisis facing the Weimar Republic reached its peak in November 1923 – but it went on to recover. For the next six years Germany went through a period of prosperity, which is sometimes called the 'golden age of the Weimar Republic'. This coincided with the influence of **Gustav Stresemann**, Chancellor for a few months in 1923 and then Foreign Minister until 1929.

Source A

▲ A German factory under full production in 1925.

Economic recovery

While Stresemann was Chancellor, the Government took action to end the inflation. The Finance Minister, Hans Luther, issued a new currency, the **Rentenmark**. This temporarily replaced the Reichsmark. Old banknotes were recalled to be destroyed.

To avoid another financial collapse in the future, other measures were introduced. In 1924 Germany agreed the **Dawes Plan** with the USA, Britain and France. This spread the load of the reparations payments according to Germany's ability to pay. The **Young Plan** (1929) extended the deadline by another 58 years. The Dawes Plan did much to restore confidence in the German economy and investment poured in, especially from the USA.

The result was quite spectacular. Between 1924 and 1929 German industry forged ahead. Factories were equipped with new machinery and German industrialists used the most successful techniques of American production. These were assembly lines, standardized patterns and interchangeable parts, all of which enabled goods to be mass-produced. The result was a much faster economic growth rate than either Britain or France. By 1929 Germany was producing 33% more than it had done in 1913, despite losing its major industrial areas under the Treaty of Versailles.

Source B

In many respects the League is the heir and executor of the treaties of 1919. Out of these treaties there have arisen in the past many differences between the League and Germany. I hope that our co-operation within the League will make it easier in future to discuss these questions. In this respect mutual confidence will be found a greater creative force than anything else.

▲ Extract from Gustav Stresemann's speech on Germany's entry into the League of Nations, 1926.

International relations

Meanwhile, Stresemann was making a vital contribution to improving Germany's position in Europe. He believed that the only way in which Germany could hope to recover its reputation was by seeking co-operation, not revenge.

The Locarno Pact

In 1925 Germany signed the **Locarno Pact**, along with France, Belgium, Britain and Italy. By this Germany, France and Belgium agreed not to attack each other or adjust each other's boundaries. Boundaries to the east were not included. In 1926 Stresemann took Germany into the League of Nations and was awarded the Nobel Peace Prize. In 1928 he signed the **Kellogg-Briand Pact**, by which over 60 countries agreed to renounce the use of war against each other in the future.

Source C

▲ Three of the statesmen who negotiated the signing of the Locarno Pact in 1925. From left to right: Stresemann, Austen Chamberlain of Britain and Aristide Briand of France.

Stresemann came in for some criticism within Germany for being too willing to co-operate with Germany's former enemies. Stresemann, however, emphasized the need for patience. He was as opposed as anyone to the Treaty of Versailles but realized that it could not be removed overnight (see Source D). This was typical of his patience and long-term view.

Political stability

The Republic was now more stable than it had been in the first five years of its existence. This was largely because Stresemann used his political skill to help the Chancellors of the time to keep the coalitions together. The result was a decline in the fortunes of the Nazi Party, which did badly in the Reichstag elections. In May 1924, the Nazis won 32 seats, followed by 14 in December 1924 and 12 in 1928. It is true that the Communists won 62 seats in May 1924, but they did less well in December 1924 and 1928. The moderate Social Democrats, on the other hand, increased their support after 1924. It seemed that the Weimar Republic was safe.

Source D

I see the importance . . . of this . . . peace between ourselves and France. It is true that these are all matters that lie in the future; a nation must not adopt the attitude of a child that writes a list of its wants on Christmas Eve, which contains everything that the child will need for the next fifteen years. The parents would not be in a position to give it all this. In foreign politics I often have the feeling that I am being confronted with such a list.

▲ An extract from a speech made by Stresemann in 1925, in which he defended his signing of the Locarno Pact against critics within Germany.

GUSTAV STRESEMANN (1878–1929)

Stresemann was leader of the National Liberal Party before 1914. This was replaced after the First World War by the German People's Party [DVP], which he also headed. From 1921, he believed that the parties should collaborate to save Germany from disintegration. He became Chancellor briefly in 1923 but his preferred post was always Foreign Minister, at which he served between 1923 and 1929. He did more than anyone else to make Germany acceptable again to the European powers, although his eventual aim was to enable Germany to get round the Treaty of Versailles. Stresemann was also an important moderating force within Germany and did much to keep Governments going during the 1920s. It was a tragedy that he died in 1929 – at a time when Germany needed his special talents.

1.7 Recovery (2): Art and culture

The 1920s saw a huge cultural revival in Germany. Indeed, these years have been seen as the greatest period of experimentation in the whole of Germany's history. As things settled down politically, writers and artists had more of a chance to try out new ideas. The results were impressive and spread across all areas of the arts.

Cultural changes

The key painters of the time produced a variety of ideas and techniques. Some, like **George Grosz**, used art to criticise society. His painting, *Grey Day*, (Source A), was a comment on the boredom experienced by most people in their everyday lives. Other artists were members of new movements. Hannah Hoech, for example, was one of the Dada school, which believed that the absurd should be considered normal. Much of her work was in the form of collage, assembled from smaller parts, including photographs. Architecture and design were profoundly affected by the new **Bauhaus** movement of Walter Gropius, with the type of result shown in Sources B and C.

Germany also became the centre for new plays and operas. The most famous playwright of the time was **Bertolt Brecht**, whose *Three-penny Opera* was an enormous success. The cinema also took huge strides. One film, the *Cabinet of Dr Calgari* was publicized as a horror film, but its real message was anti-military and anti-war. Literature was dominated by Arnold Zweig, Hermann Hesse, Stefan George, Thomas Mann and **Erich Remarque**. The last of these wrote the celebrated anti-war novel, *All Quiet on the Western Front*. This novel described the horrors and destruction of the First World War. Within three months of its publication in 1929, it had sold 500,000 copies. Later, it was dramatized and made into a highly successful film.

Source A

◀ ***Grey Day* by George Grosz, a comment on everyday life in Germany.**

Source B

▶ **The sculpture workshop of the Bauhaus Group, (which was founded by Walter Gropius) in a building designed by Gropius in Dessau.**

Lively debate flourished in the atmosphere of completely free expression allowed by the Republic. At the centre of this hectic activity was Berlin, with its 120 newspapers and periodicals and 40 theatres. One German writer, Thomas Mann, claimed with some justification that Germany had replaced France as the cultural centre of Europe. He might also have added that Berlin had replaced Paris.

Opposition to these changes

Criticism came from several quarters. People on the right wing – whether in the Nazi Party or the DNVP – considered that what was being produced in the Weimar Republic was 'decadent' and unpatriotic. The new culture did not represent the more traditional virtues of Germany. The far left wing, especially the Communists, felt that experimentation was a luxury and did not reflect the real needs of the working class. Between the two extremes were many ordinary people in Germany who were confused by the rapid changes in culture. They were not impressed when they saw the paintings of Grosz, or the new buildings or furniture of Gropius. Many also blamed the new wave of art for a decline of moral standards in the 1920s. Berlin had a huge number of night clubs and there was more emphasis on sex in entertainment than in Paris. Some people reacted prudishly to this; others were genuinely worried.

The culture of the Weimar Republic later became a target for the Nazis during the period of the Third Reich. They attacked it as '**degenerate**' and 'un-German'. But, for the moment, it was all new, exciting and adventurous – and it was a means by which Germany came again to influence Europe.

Source C

▲ The exterior of the Einstein Tower in Potsdam, near Berlin. This was designed by Erich Mendelsohn and named in honour of the famous physicist.

Source D

▲ A scene from the *Three-penny Opera* written by Bertolt Brecht in 1928.

WALTER GROPIUS (1883–1969)

Gropius was born in Berlin during the period of the Second Reich. He studied architecture and, after the First World War, became the most influential of all the leaders of the fine arts. He developed a new form, known as Bauhaus, which applied especially to buildings and furniture. He used bold designs and unusual materials. He had many critics within Germany and when Hitler came to power his works were declared degenerate. He was forced to leave Germany in 1934, moving first to London, then to the USA. He eventually became an American citizen and professor of architecture at Harvard, the USA's leading university.

QUESTIONS

1. Describe how Stresemann helped Germany recover in the years 1923–29.
2. Describe German art and culture in the years 1923–29.
3. Were the years 1923–29 really ones of 'recovery'?

1.8 Why did crisis return to the Republic 1929–33?

In 1929 the golden age of Weimar came to an abrupt end. The reason was another crisis which eventually killed democracy within the Republic – and then the Republic itself. This crisis had two related parts. The first was economic collapse, which led directly to the second – political problems which proved impossible to overcome.

Economic crisis

German recovery after the inflation of 1923 had been brought about largely by American investment, a direct result of the Dawes Plan of 1924. There was, however, a hitch. The investment was in the form of short-term loans which could be ended at any time and repayment demanded in full. For most of the 1920s, the American economy had expanded rapidly and investors were happy to renew loans to Germany as they were needed. But, in October 1929, disaster struck the New York stock exchange on Wall Street. The value of shares collapsed following a few days of wild speculation. Many business people were ruined. The Americans had no option but to pull out their investments from Germany and demand immediate repayment.

Year	Numbers unemployed
1928	1.8
1929	2.9
1930	3.2
1931	4.9
1932	6.0

▲ **Unemployment in Germany 1928–32 (in millions).**

This destroyed the whole basis of Germany's recovery. Thousands of businesses went bankrupt, deprived of the money which had kept them going. To make matters worse, most countries in the world slid into a **depression** as overseas markets for their goods suddenly declined. This meant that even those German businesses which had managed without loans were also badly affected. Large numbers of workers had

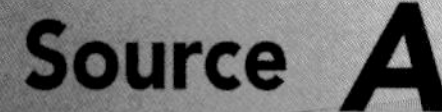

Source A

No one knew how many there were of them. They completely filled the streets. They stood or lay about in the streets as if they had taken root there. They sat or lay on the pavements or in the roadway and gravely shared out scraps of newspapers among themselves.

▲ **Description, in a short story, of the suffering in Germany caused by the depression.**

Source B

▶ **Unemployed people in Hanover queue to receive their dole money, 1932.**

to be laid off and the number of unemployed in Germany increased rapidly, reaching six million by 1932. The result was social misery on a huge scale, which affected all classes. Many people had to give up their homes since they could no longer afford the rent on them. Instead, they had to move into makeshift dwellings in shanty towns, and the streets became filled with people who had no work and no hope. The suffering seemed particularly bad since the German people, especially the middle class, had so recently experienced prosperity. The memory of the earlier economic crisis of 1919–23 returned, leaving many people doubly bitter.

Political crisis

Economic crises nearly always produce political crises, because governments suddenly find themselves having to deal with an impossible situation. This is what happened from 1929 onwards.

We have seen that democracy in Germany depended on the co-operation of parties in coalition governments. This was because the Constitution provided for elections by proportional representation which meant that no single party ever had an overall majority in the Reichstag. In good times this worked well, and Stresemann had managed to patch up differences between party leaders. In 1929, however, the two leading partners in the coalition, the Centre Party and the SPD fell out with each other. The leader of the SPD, **Hermann Müller**, refused to agree to cuts in unemployment benefit which the Centre Party, under **Heinrich Brüning**, argued were essential in the circumstances. Brüning and the Centre Party therefore found themselves in government alone.

The slide to dictatorship

Between 1929 and 1931 Brüning tried to keep his government going without a majority in the Reichstag. The only way he could do this was to ask the President to use Article 48 of the Constitution. This meant that laws could be issued under emergency powers rather than having to go through the Reichstag. The President was **Paul von Hindenburg**, elected in 1925 following the death of Ebert. He was sympathetic to the right wing and impatient with democracy. This meant that he was willing to use Article 48 regularly, whereas the original intention was that it should be used only occasionally. Between 1930–2 the Reichstag sat less frequently and became more and more helpless. The situation became more serious between 1932 and 1933. Brüning was successively replaced as Chancellor by, **Franz von Papen** and **Kurt von Schleicher**, who were not attached to any party but who wanted to end democracy in the Republic.

Year	Decrees issued
1930	5
1931	44
1932	60

▲ **The number of decrees issued under Article 48 of the Constitution, 1930–32.**

Year	Times Reichstag sat
1930	94
1931	41
1932	13

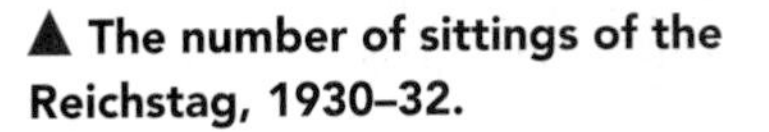

▲ **The number of sittings of the Reichstag, 1930–32.**

Source C

The one consolation could be the recognition that the National Socialists [Nazis] have passed their peak, since . . . they have declined in most constituencies, but against this stands the fact that the radicalism of the right has unleashed a strong radicalism on the left. The Communists have made gains almost everywhere.

▲ **An extract from a memorandum by Dr Kulz, Minister of the Interior in 1932. He is referring to the Reichstag election of July 1932.**

They were also given full use of Article 48 by President Hindenburg. An additional complication was that Papen and Schleicher were bitter personal rivals. Schleicher brought about Papen's fall in 1932, while Papen persuaded Hindenburg to remove Schleicher in 1933 by appointing a new Chancellor, Adolf Hitler, with Papen as Deputy Chancellor. Although Hitler's support had grown after 1930, the Nazis had lost some of their seats in the second election of 1932. Papen and Hindenburg therefore assumed that Hitler had passed his peak and could be manipulated to do what they wanted. This was, of course, the most disastrous error of judgement.

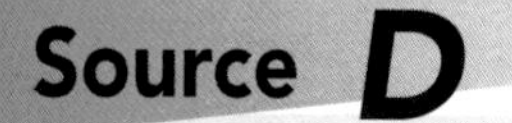

▲ **A collage by the German artist, John Heartfield, showing what happened to the Weimar Republic. Ebert is the caterpillar, Hindenburg the chrysalis, and Hitler the butterfly. (A chrysalis is the middle stage in the life cycle of a butterfly.)**

Why did democracy collapse in the Weimar Republic?

Democracy in the Weimar Republic was always fragile because of the strength of conservative influences and attacks from the extreme left and extreme right. It also had to struggle against external pressures and economic collapse.

At first it managed to survive and even prosper. This was because of the skill of Stresemann and the investment from the USA. But the second economic crisis of 1929 shattered this recovery and things went wrong politically. Coalition government collapsed and the last three chancellors (Brüning, Papen and Schleicher) used the emergency powers of President Hindenburg. Article 48 of the Constitution, which had been intended to save democracy in times of need, was now used as a weapon against democracy.

QUESTIONS

1. Which is more useful to explain the problem of unemployment in Germany – the statistics on pages 18–19 or Sources A and B? Explain your answer.
2. Explain the connection between the two charts on page 19.
3. Why did economic crisis lead to political crisis after 1929?
4. What is the meaning of Source D? Is it an accurate view of how Hitler became Chancellor?

What kind of dictatorship?

Events after 1929 all pointed towards the growth of dictatorship in Germany. But this did not have to mean the rise of Hitler. It is quite possible that Germany might have experienced an **authoritarian** system, or a dictatorship under conservative forces similar to those in the Second Reich. What actually happened was the growth of a **totalitarian** dictatorship which controlled all areas of people's lives. This was quite new and was the work of Hitler alone. We now need to explain why Hitler's Party was in a position to take advantage of the crisis of 1929–33.

A PRESIDENT AND THREE CHANCELLORS

The President: Paul von Hindenburg (1847–1934)

Hindenburg was a member of the Prussian aristocratic landowning class [known as Junkers]. Like many Junkers, he had a military career and retired in 1911 at the age of 64, not suspecting how much more still lay ahead for him. He was recalled to command the German armies in the First World War, along with Ludendorff. He benefited greatly from the 'stab in the back' propaganda put out after 1919 by the right-wing parties, since most of the blame for losing the war came to be attached to the Government rather than to the army. Hindenburg became Germany's most popular elder statesman and, in 1925, was elected President. He was re-elected in 1932. Hindenburg did not belong to any particular party, although he was more sympathetic to the DNVP than the others. He was impatient of the workings of democracy and he allowed the Weimar Republic to slide towards dictatorship after 1930. He was too willing to use his emergency powers under Article 48 of the Constitution. He appointed Hitler Chancellor in January 1933, thinking that Hitler could be controlled. Hindenburg died in 1934, after which his position as President was taken by Hitler, who then became Führer.

Source E

▲ **A poster of Paul von Hindenburg, President of Germany, 1925–34.**

Chancellor 1: Heinrich Brüning (1885–1970)

Brüning was the leader of the Centre Party from 1929. He tried to keep the Republic afloat but found it more and more difficult to get the support of the Reichstag. Instead of resigning, he made use of Hindenburg's powers under Article 48 of the Constitution to rule by decree. When Hitler came to power, he left Germany.

Chancellor 2: Franz von Papen (1879–1969)

For much of his earlier career Papen was a diplomat, before joining the Centre Party. He then moved further to the right and, like Schleicher and Hindenburg, was impatient with the Republic. In order to keep Schleicher out of government he was prepared to do a deal with Hitler in 1933.

Chancellor 3: Kurt von Schleicher (1882–1934)

Like Hindenburg, Schleicher was a Prussian who served on the German General Staff during the First World War. He hated democracy and sought every opportunity to destroy the Weimar Republic. But he also disliked Papen and refused to co-operate with him. Schleicher was eventually killed on Hitler's orders in 1934.

Source F

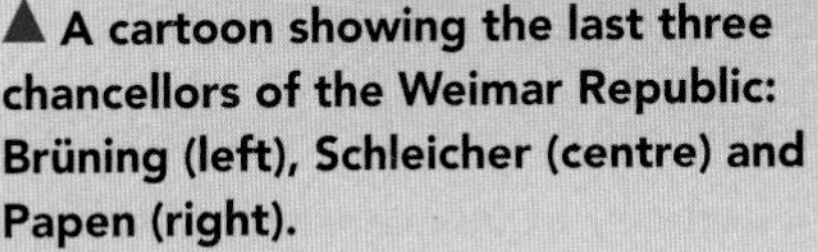

▲ **A cartoon showing the last three chancellors of the Weimar Republic: Brüning (left), Schleicher (centre) and Papen (right).**

SUMMARY

- **1918** Military and naval mutinies. Scheidemann proclaimed Germany a Republic. Germany surrendered to the Allies
- **1919** Spartacist uprising in Berlin. First Reichstag meeting in Weimar. Signing of Treaty of Versailles. New constitution adopted.
- **1920** Kapp *Putsch*.
- **1921** Amount of reparations announced.
- **1923** French occupation of the Ruhr. Peak of inflation. Hitler's Munich *Putsch*.
- **1924** Dawes Plan.
- **1925** Hindenburg elected President. Stresemann signed the Locarno Pact (October).
- **1926** Germany allowed to join the League of Nations.
- **1928** Stresemann signed Kellogg-Briand Pact.
- **1929** Young Plan: settlement of reparations. Death of Stresemann. Wall Street Crash.
- **1930–1** Brüning used Hindenburg's emergency powers.
- **1932** Rivalry between Papen and Schleicher.
- **1933** Hitler appointed Chancellor (January).

1.9 Exercise: The Weimar Republic 1919–33

Source 1

So it had all been in vain. In vain all the sacrifices. In vain the hours in which, with mortal fear clutching at our hearts we did our duty. In vain the death of two millions. Had they died for this, so that a gang of wretched criminals could lay hands on the fatherland?

▲ **Hitler, writing in *Mein Kampf*, about Germany's First World War surrender in November 1918. Hitler wrote *Mein Kampf* ('My Struggle') when he was in prison, following the failure of the Munich *Putsch* of 1923. It told the story of his life so far and explained his ideas. It was first published in 1925.**

Source 2

By the death of Herr Stresemann, Germany has lost her ablest politician. Stresemann worked for the rebuilding of his shattered country. When he became Chancellor, Germany was in ruins. The French were in the Ruhr and the problem of reparations hung over a bankrupt Germany which was seething with unrest. He had extremists to the right and left to obstruct him at every turn. Germany is now orderly and prosperous and has a new standing in the affairs of Europe.

▲ **An obituary of Stresemann which appeared in the British newspaper *The Times*, 4 October 1929. Stresemann died on 3 October 1929.**

1 a In Source 1, Hitler calls the leaders of the Weimar Republic 'wretched criminals'. What crime had they committed in Hitler's eyes?

b How reliable is Source 1 for historians studying the Weimar Republic?

2 Why does Source 2 claim that Germany was 'in ruins' when Stresemann came to power in 1923?

3 Source 2 is an interpretation of the importance of Stresemann in stabilizing Weimar Germany. Looking back over this chapter, how accurate is this interpretation of Stresemann's success?

4 It has been argued that Stresemann's death was a tragedy for Germany. Using your knowledge of the period 1919–33, do you agree or disagree with this view?

CHAPTER 2

THE RISE OF HITLER TO 1933

Hitler was appointed Chancellor by President Hindenburg in January 1933. As we have already seen, this was due partly to the crisis experienced by the Weimar Republic after 1929 which saw a drift towards dictatorship. It was, however, also due to the contribution made by Hitler himself to converting the Nazi Party from a tiny and insignificant party in 1919 to the largest party in the Reichstag by 1932.

2.1 How did Hitler come to dominate the Nazi Party?

Source A

▲ **The beer cellar in Munich where the first meetings of the Nazi Party were held.**

Source B

Our little committee, which with its seven members in reality represented the whole party, was nothing but the managing committee of a small whist club. . . . To start with, we met in a pathetic little room in a small pub . . . The committee's proceedings consisted in reading out letters received, discussing replies to them, and registering the letters that were sent off following this discussion.

▲ **Hitler's description in 1929 of the meetings of the German Workers' Party (DAP) in 1919.**

The situation in Bavaria 1918–23

Like all the German states, Bavaria had its own government. At the end of 1918 and the beginning of 1919 this was, for a few months, controlled by far-left revolutionaries. They declared Bavaria a communist republic, thus achieving what the Spartacists had tried and failed to do in Berlin. But this success was short-lived. President Ebert ordered the ***Freikorps***, the troops which had destroyed the Spartacists and shot its leaders, to move south and clean out Munich, the capital city of Bavaria. They placed in power a government which was loyal to the Weimar Republic.

Then, in 1920, another change took place. While Berlin was going through the upheaval of the Kapp *Putsch*, Munich experienced its own revolt. A right-wing group seized power in Munich and a new Bavarian state government was set up under **Gustav von Kahr**.

These developments were important. The Nazi Party started and grew in Bavaria and benefited greatly from the right-wing atmosphere which existed in Munich from 1920 onwards.

The foundation of a new party

The Nazi Party was originally called the German Workers' Party (or DAP). It was founded in Munich in January 1919 by **Anton Drexler**, a railway mechanic, and was joined by Adolf Hitler in September 1919.

At the time there was nothing remarkable either about the DAP or about Hitler. The party was one of many small racialist groups springing up in the unstable conditions of post-war Germany. Drexler had no apparent ambition for the party except as a discussion and correspondence group. Hitler was a failed Austrian architect who had lived rough in Vienna before joining the German army in 1914. The end of the war saw Hitler in hospital in Munich recovering from gas-poisoning and also nursing a burning hatred of the new Republic. On joining the DAP he quickly showed a talent for public speaking and propaganda and rose quickly up the ranks of the party. In February 1920 he and Drexler put forward the **Twenty-Five Point Programme** of the DAP (see page 28) and Hitler was placed in charge of propaganda. He was also responsible for two other developments in 1920. One was the purchase of a newspaper, the *Münchener Beobachter*, (the *Munich Observer*). The other was a change in the name of the party to **National Socialist German Workers' Party** or NSDAP (abbreviated to Nazi).

Source C

The new movement aimed at providing what the others did not: a racialist movement with a firm social base, a hold over the broad masses, welded together in an iron-hard organization, instilled with blind obedience and inspired by a brutal will.

▲ Hitler describes how the Nazi movement differs from other parties. Taken from an internal party memorandum of 7 January 1922.

Hitler takes over the leadership

In 1921 Hitler was strong enough to challenge Drexler and take over the leadership of the Party himself. He then put across a very different vision of the future. The Party would become the spearhead of a mass movement and would be far more aggressive than it had ever been under Drexler. All the time Hitler was asserting himself as a magnetic speaker with the power to captivate his audiences. He was already regarded within the movement as the **Führer** and his followers owed him their absolute allegiance and obedience.

Source D

My critical faculty was swept away. Leaning from the rostrum as if he were trying to impel his inner self into the consciousness of all these thousands, he was holding the masses, and me with them, under an hypnotic spell by the sheer force of his conviction . . . I forgot everything but the man; then glancing around, I saw that his magnetism was holding these thousands as one.

▲ Kurt Ludecke describes how he was affected by one of Hitler's speeches in 1922.

Hitler and the SA

In August 1921 Hitler set about converting the Nazi Party into a mass movement. He organized a series of armed groups under the title 'Gymnastic and Sports Sections', a name which was intended as a camouflage. In October he changed the name to *Sturm Abteilung* (SA) or Stormtroopers. The SA attracted many ex-soldiers. Particularly enthusiastic were the *Freikorps*, who had been used by the Government to put down the Spartacists in Berlin, but who were disbanded in 1920 because of their connection with the Kapp *Putsch*. Many of these ex-soldiers found the SA their natural home and they enjoyed the enormous feeling of power it gave them.

The SA was a **paramilitary** group, who paraded in brown uniforms and carried swastika banners. Members undertook total obedience to the SA leadership, to the Nazi movement and to Hitler himself (Source F). They were employed to break up the meetings of other parties, especially those held by the Communists and Social Democrats. There were frequent brawls and many injuries. There is no doubt that the activities of the SA gave Hitler the confidence to take the next step – an attempt to seize power.

The Munich *Putsch*: events

On 8 November 1923 a meeting being addressed by Gustav von Kahr, the head of the Bavarian Government, was suddenly interrupted by a Nazi demonstration. The hall was surrounded by SA men, and Hitler burst in brandishing a revolver. He announced that he was taking over the government of Bavaria (as Kahr had done in 1920). The next stage, he said, would be a march on Berlin to take over the German Government. He tried to persuade Kahr to support him but the latter said nothing. Kahr was locked in a room, from which he managed to escape sometime during the night.

Source E

▲ **The SA displaying the swastika. The words on the flag say, 'Germany awake'.**

Hitler tried again the following day, with about 3,000 supporters, some of whom were SA men. This time he was met by armed police called out by Kahr to break up the march. Sixteen of the marchers were killed when the police opened fire but Hitler stayed in the background. Later he was caught and put on trial for treason.

The Munich *Putsch*: reasons

Hitler clearly wanted to destroy the Weimar Republic and thought he could succeed where Kahr had failed. He was also greatly encouraged by Mussolini's success in taking power in Italy as a result of his so-called **March on Rome** in 1922. Hitler was convinced that the Republic had been fatally wounded by the hyper-inflation of 1923 and by the French invasion of the Ruhr. Besides, he was fairly confident that he would receive the support of Kahr, who had no reason to support the Republic.

Source F

As a member of the storm troop of the NSDAP, I pledge myself by its storm flag: to be always ready to stake life and limb in the struggle for the aims of the movement; to give absolute military obedience to my military superiors and leaders; to bear myself honourably in and out of service.

▲ **The pledge of loyalty and obedience taken by members of the SA.**

The Munich *Putsch*: the outcome

Unfortunately for Hitler, Kahr preferred not to commit himself to any wild schemes at this stage. Hitler therefore failed to win his support, or the sympathy of the army and the police. In February 1924 he was put on trial and Kahr appeared as one of the witnesses for the prosecution. The whole affair could have been a humiliating failure. But Hitler turned his trial into a propaganda success. He used the occasion to attack the Republic and to claim that he had only been acting as a patriotic German. When Hitler eventually came to power, the Munich *Putsch* was presented to the German people as an heroic event.

In April the court found Hitler guilty of treason. It could hardly have done otherwise since the evidence was overwhelming. Yet the court was also sympathetic to Hitler. Instead of sentencing him to death as it might have done, it gave him the minimum sentence for the offence – five years imprisonment. The judges also made it clear that he could expect an early release.

In fact, Hitler served just nine months of his sentence. He was confined to Landsberg Prison but in special conditions. He was allowed as many visitors as he wished and he spent much of the time dictating the first part of his book, *Mein Kampf* ('My Struggle'). Imprisonment provided Hitler with a period of enforced leisure in which he was able to sort out his main ideas.

Source G

We wanted to create in Germany the precondition which alone will make it possible for the iron grip of our enemies to be removed from us. We wanted to create order in the state, throw out the drones, take up the fight against international stock exchange slavery . . . and above all, for the highest honourable duty which we, as Germans, know should be once more introduced – the duty of bearing arms, military service. And now I ask you: Is what we wanted high treason?

▲ **Hitler's defence at his trial in Munich, February 1924.**

Source H

▲ **A painting, produced in 1933, after Hitler came to power, of Hitler preparing for the Munich *Putsch*.**

QUESTIONS

1. What changes did Hitler make to the German Workers' Party?
2. Using Sources E and F on page 25 and the text, explain the purpose and importance of the SA.
3. Did the Munich *Putsch* have the intended outcome for the Nazis? Explain your answer.
4. Was the Munich *Putsch* a failure for Hitler and the Nazis? Explain your answer.
5. What was the artist's intention in Source H? How is this shown in the source?

2.2 What were Hitler's main ideas?

The sources

Hitler wrote comparatively little, compared with other 20th century leaders like Lenin. Nevertheless, he did leave two books containing his main beliefs. The first was *Mein Kampf* ('My Struggle'), written during his imprisonment in 1924. The second was kept secret during his lifetime and not published until 1959. It is usually called the *Zweites Buch* ('Second Book'). There are also transcripts of speeches and conversations, together with official Party documents and programmes.

Source A

▲ Burning of Jews in medieval Germany (from Schedal's *Chronicle*).

The background

Hitler's ideas were not new. Most of Hitler's beliefs had been held by people in the past. In Europe throughout the Middle Ages there had been violent **anti-Semitism**, or hatred of the Jews. This had continued in some sections of society well into the modern period. It even influenced Hitler's favourite composer, Richard Wagner (1813–83), who wrote a book called *Judaism in Music*.

There was also a long-standing belief in the master race and the superman: Hitler would certainly have read the sort of pamphlet shown in Source B. During the 19th century Charles Darwin had developed the theory of evolution in his work, *Origin of Species*. Part of his argument was that some species of plants and animals learned to adapt and survive, while others became extinct. This theory was picked up by non-scientists, who applied it to human beings. The '**Social Darwinists**', as they came to be called, believed that some races were superior to others, and that this was the result of a long and continuing struggle. An example was Ernst Haeckel (1834–1919), a famous German scientist and philospher. All the components were there before Hitler came to power but he blended them into a new ideology: National Socialism, or **Nazism**.

Source B

Are You Blond?
If so, You are
A CULTURE–
CREATOR
and
CULTURE–
SUPPORTER

▲ The title page of a pamphlet written by J. Lanz-Liebenfels and published in 1913.

The party programme: Nationalism and Socialism

The first official description of the policy of the German Workers' Party (DAP) was the *Twenty-Five Point Programme* of 1920 (see Source C on page 28). This programme contained policies which may be described as either **nationalist** or **socialist** or both. The nationalist policies emphasized race, expansion, the army, power, and relations with other countries. The socialist policies were to do with state controls over the living conditions of the people and the economy.

Source C

1 We demand the union of all Germans in a Greater Germany.
2 We demand equality of rights for the German people in its dealings with other nations.
3 We demand land and colonies to feed our people and to settle our surplus population.
4 Only those of German blood . . . may be members of the nation. No Jew may be a member of the nation.

• • •

7 We demand that the State shall make it its primary duty to provide a livelihood for its citizens.
8 All non-German immigration must be prevented.
9 All citizens shall have equal rights and duties.
10 It must be the first duty of every citizen to perform mental or physical work.
11 We demand the abolition of incomes unearned by work.
12 Personal enrichment from war must be regarded as a crime against the nation. We demand therefore the ruthless confiscation of all war profits.
13 We demand the nationalization of all businesses which have been formed into corporations.
14 We demand profit-sharing in large industrial enterprises.
15 We demand the extensive development of insurance for old age.
16 We demand . . . the immediate communalising of big department stores.
17 We demand a land reform suitable to our national requirement.

• • •

21 The State must ensure that the nation's health standards are raised by protecting mothers and infants.
22 We demand . . . the formation of a people's army.
23 The publishing of newspapers which are not conducive to the national welfare must be forbidden.

• • •

25 We demand the creation of a strong central state power for the Reich.

◀ **Extracts from the Twenty-Five Point Programme of the Nazi Party. It was originally drawn up by the DAP in February 1920.**

Race, struggle and conquest

Hitler soon extended the range of his ideas, going well beyond the statements made in the Party Programme. His speeches were full of Social Darwinism and contained numerous references to struggles between strong and weak (see Source E). The strong now became the 'culture creators', with a duty to overcome the 'culture destroyers'. Hitler took this further still. The Germans, or **Aryans**, were the master race and should prepare for expansion against the 'inferior' races of eastern Europe. This would mean military conquest, the most extreme form of Social Darwinism. The 'superman' type who would accomplish this became more and more stereotyped, with blond hair and blue eyes.

Source D

Now one can say that the struggle for existence is the 'survival of the fittest' or the 'victory of the best', but one can do that only if one assumes that the fittest are necessarily, and in a moral sense, the best . . . Thousands of good and beautiful and admirable species of animals and plants have perished during those forty-eight million years, because they had to make room for other and stronger species . . . Precisely the same applies to the history of nations.

▲ **From a book by Ernst Haeckel, published in 1900. Haeckel believed in 'Social Darwinism'.**

Source E

It has always been the right of the stronger, before God and man, to see his will prevail. All of nature is one great struggle between strength and weakness, an eternal victory of the strong over the weak.

▲ **An extract from a speech by Hitler in 1923.**

Anti-Semitism

Hatred of the Jews was Hitler's greatest obsession. Although anti-Semitism was not new, Hitler took it to its extreme form.

Hitler considered Jews to be the lowest of the 'inferior' races; in fact, he described them in *Mein Kampf* as 'race polluters'. They were responsible for all the ills in society – for economic exploitation, for unemployment and for all forms of corruption. The full list of their alleged activities can be seen in Source F. Jews were accused of being **capitalist** exploiters *and* communist revolutionaries. Hitler explained the contradiction in this by saying that Jewish plots changed shape according to the circumstances. Hence the Weimar Republic was a 'Jew Republic' and the army had been 'stabbed in the back' in November 1918 by a government inspired by Jews.

Hitler's overall message was very compelling. Ordinary Germans were part of a master race and had every right to take what they needed from other races. All their problems could be blamed on 'inferior' races, and especially the Jews. It was a new and lethal combination of old prejudices.

QUESTIONS

1 a Why does the author of Source D think that 'thousands of species have perished'?

b What does he think will happen to some nations?

2 How do Sources E, G and H support the ideas in Source D?

3 Expain the method used to put across anti-Jewish ideas in Source F.

4 Study Source C. Which of the aims do you think were 'nationalist' and which were 'socialist'? Give reasons for your choice.

5 Was the Nazi Party democratic in any way? Explain your answer.

Source F

THE ANTI-SEMITES WANT TO INCITE YOU

Workers, Citizens, Soldiers, Women!
SUPPORT US! for:
Who are the big capitalists . . . ?
We Jews!

Who has a greater annual income than Krupp's fortune?
We Jews!

Who led and paid the Spartacists and the Bolsheviks?
We Jews!

Who is a united race amongst a divided . . . people?
We Jews!

Who offers you truly licentious [obscene] art in the cinema, cabaret and theatre and wants Christian morality to go to the devil?
We Jews!

▲ **From a Nazi leaflet, printed in 1922.**

Source G

All great cultures of the past were destroyed only because the originally creative race died from blood poisoning . . . Therefore, he who would live, let him fight, and he who would not fight in this world of struggle is not deserving of life.

▲ **Extracts from Hitler's *Mein Kampf*, 1925.**

Source H

Germany resolves to change to a clear, far-sighted policy of expansion. It shall thus turn away from all attempts at world trade and international industrial enterprise, and instead concentrate all its forces on providing our nation with sufficient living space. Such space can only be in the east.

▲ **An extract from Hitler's *Second Book*, written in 1928, but not published until 1959.**

The change of strategy

While he was in Landsberg Prison, Hitler began to work out a new strategy for changing Germany in the future. He had always assumed that he would come to power as a result of a revolution and that he could then introduce the changes he wanted, based on the ideas described on page 28. The failure of the Munich *Putsch* meant that he would have to win power legally through elections. He realized he would now have to compete with the other parties for the support of the electorate. Once he had gained power, however, he would be able to use the Constitution of the Weimar Republic against itself, to destroy democracy. Hitler therefore reversed his whole approach. The Nazi revolution would be introduced after he had come to power, and not be the means by which he would achieve power.

Source A

When I pursue active work, it will be necessary to pursue a new policy. Instead of working to achieve power by an armed coup, we will have to hold our noses and enter the Reichstag against Catholic and Marxist members. If outvoting them takes longer than outshooting them, at least the result will be guaranteed by their own Constitution. Sooner or later we shall have a majority, and after that – Germany!

▲ **From a letter written by Hitler while in Landsberg Prison in 1924.**

Refounding the Party

The Nazi Party had fallen into decline while Hitler was in prison. Hitler was not worried by this as it showed the party needed him. He realized that no one was likely to replace him as he had replaced Drexler.

Nevertheless, on his release in December 1924, he immediately set about reorganizing the Party. Branches were set up all over Germany and each regional organization (or *Gau*) was placed under the control of a Party official called the ***Gauleiter***. Hitler soon came up against a possible threat. The Nazis of northern Germany, under **Joseph Goebbels** and **Gregor Strasser**, wanted to make the Nazi programme more and more socialist and to concentrate on gaining more support from the working class. Hitler called a Party Conference at **Bamberg**, in Bavaria, in 1926. There he won over Goebbels and Strasser by the power of his arguments. From that time onwards Goebbels became an unquestioning supporter, and was immediately rewarded by being made *Gauleiter* of Berlin.

More attention was also given to the SA and to increasing the proportion of younger men both in the movement and the Party.

Source B

Characteristic of this period was the steady disappearance of all leaders and subordinate leaders whose views and methods of struggle were still rooted in pre-war days. Their places were taken by the young men of what was known as the front generation of 25–35 years old.

▲ **The recollections of Albert Krebs, *Gauleiter* in Hamburg.**

How successful were the Nazis in this period?

There are two ways of looking at this question. On the one hand, the Nazis had considerable success. The Party's organization was greatly improved and the Nazi propaganda machine was far more effective after 1925 than it had ever been up to 1923.

Source C

▲ A Nazi election poster of 1928. It says that the sacrifices made by Germany in the First World War were in vain.

Source D

The election results from the rural areas in particular have proved that with a smaller expenditure of energy, money and time, better results can be achieved there than in the big cities.

▲ From the Nazi newspaper the *Munich Observer*, 31 May 1928, eleven days after the Reichstag election.

Source E

This is the great secret of our movement: an utter devotion to the idea of National Socialism, a glowing faith in the victorious strength of this doctrine of liberation and deliverance, is combined with a deep love of the person of our leader who is the shining hero of the new freedom fighters.

▲ A glowing description of Hitler in an article written by Gregor Strasser in 1927. Strasser was later to come into conflict with Hitler, and was murdered by the SS in 1934.

One of Hitler's new converts, Joseph Goebbels, made a considerable impact in the propaganda field (Source C shows the type of poster being produced during this period). The Nazis had also become a nationwide party and were no longer confined to Bavaria. In addition, they were gaining support from groups which had previously ignored them, such as farmers and skilled craftsmen. By 1928, therefore, they were no longer merely a party for the working class. Above all, they had the leadership of Hitler himself. In many ways, the Nazis were well placed for a popular breakthrough.

On the other hand, the breakthrough had not come by 1928. The Nazis continued to perform badly in the elections to the Reichstag, as the chart shows.

Date	Nazi seats	Number of parties with more seats
1924 [May]	32	5
1924 [Dec.]	14	7
1928	12	7

▲ The Nazi Party's performance in Reichstag elections, 1924–8.

This is mainly explained by the German people being more contented between 1924 and 1929, because of the economic prosperity of the Stresemann era (see pages 14–15). Most voters supported the moderate parties – the Centre Party (Z), the Social Democrats (SPD) and the People's Party (DVP). It would therefore take a major upheaval to turn the Nazi Party into an election winner.

This is precisely what happened in 1929.

Source A

▲ ***Our Last Hope: Hitler*, a Nazi poster of 1932.**

Hitler's path to power

We have already seen on pages 18–19 that the Weimar Republic suffered an economic crisis and gradually abandoned democracy between 1929 and 1933. During this period, the Nazis greatly increased their hold on the electorate. In 1928 they had only 12 seats in the Reichstag and were the eighth largest party. In 1930 this number went up to 107, making them second to the Social Democrats (SPD). In the two elections of 1932 (held in July and November), they were clearly the largest party, winning 230 and then 196 seats.

Hitler felt that his earlier change of tactics was working well and he aimed for the top political post in Germany. In March 1932 he challenged Hindenburg for the presidency, but lost by 19.4 million votes to 13.4 million. He then set his sights on the second post. This he achieved when Hindenburg, the President, appointed him Chancellor in January 1933. This was made possible because of the bitter rivalry between the last two Chancellors – Papen and Schleicher. Papen persuaded Hindenburg to appoint Hitler largely to keep Schleicher out.

Throughout 1931 and 1932 Hitler campaigned vigorously. He showed his talents as a speaker to the full and had the crowds in ecstasy. He toured Germany by air, something the other party leaders never bothered to do, and he spoke in halls and sports stadia. Loudspeakers relayed his speeches to people outside, and there were always spectacular processions and marches.

Source B

The victory of the national socialist movement will mean the overcoming of the old class and caste spirit. It will allow a nation once more to rise out of status mania and class madness. It will train the nation to have iron determination. It will overcome democracy and reassert the authority of personality.

▲ **From the *Nazi Party Manifesto*, 1930.**

The nature of Hitler's appeal

Hitler's success was undoubtedly due to the Great Depression. Yet the Nazi Party made the most of the situation and appealed to the German people at two levels:

1 It appealed to the whole nation, on issues which concerned everyone.
2 It also appealed to sectors of the population, on issues which affected them separately.

These might be described as *national* and *sectoral* appeals.

The national appeal of the Nazis

The Nazis took their stand on three major issues which affected the whole population.

- First, they revived talk of the 'stab in the back' of 1918 and betrayal through the Treaty of Versailles of 1919. This was very important. One of the reasons that the Nazis had not done well before 1929 was that Stresemann had calmed down German resentment against the Allies. By reviving the demands for revenge the Nazis undermined the moderate feeling that Stresemann had helped to create.
- Second, Hitler exploited the Great Depression and the suffering it caused. He blamed the policies of the Republic for bringing it about and put across the Nazi Party as Germany's last hope. In doing this, he emphasized that, under his leadership, the Nazi Party would unite the German people in this time of crisis, whereas the other parties would only divide them.

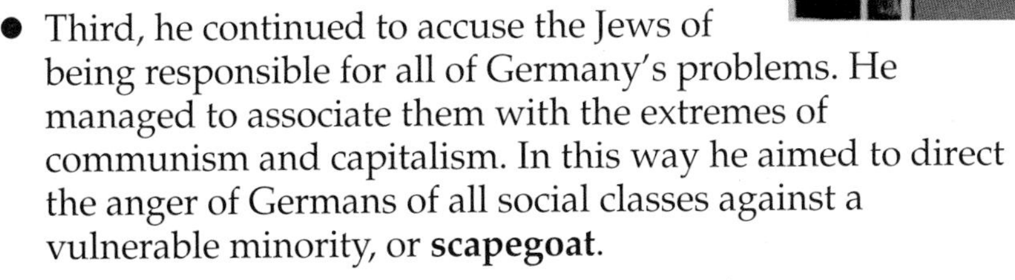

- Third, he continued to accuse the Jews of being responsible for all of Germany's problems. He managed to associate them with the extremes of communism and capitalism. In this way he aimed to direct the anger of Germans of all social classes against a vulnerable minority, or **scapegoat**.

Source C

▲ **A Nazi anti-Jewish poster, published before Hitler came to power in 1933.**

Source D

The National Socialist movement, assembled at this hour, as a fighting squad around its leader, today calls on the entire German people to join its ranks, and to pave a path that will bring Adolf Hitler to the head of the nation and thus

Lead Germany to Freedom

Hitler is the password of all who believe in Germany's resurrection. Hitler is the last hope of those who were deprived of everything: of farm and home, of savings, unemployment, survival.

. . . Hitler is the word of deliverance for millions, for they are in despair.

Hitler was bequeathed the legacy of two million dead comrades of the World War, who died not for the present system of the gradual destruction of our nation, but for Germany's future.

HITLER WILL WIN, BECAUSE THE PEOPLE WANT HIS VICTORY!

▲ **An article from the *Munich Observer*, March 1932, supporting Hitler in the presidential elections.**

Source E

GERMAN FARMER YOU BELONG TO HITLER! WHY?

The German farmer stands in between two great dangers today: The one danger is the American economic system–Big capitalism! The other is the Marxist economic system of BOLSHEVISM. Big Capitalism and Bolshevism work hand in hand: they are born of Jewish thought and serve the master plan of world Jewry. Who alone can rescue the farmer from these dangers? NATIONAL SOCIALISM.

▲ **From a Nazi leaflet, 1932.**

Source F

▲ **A Nazi Party poster, claiming that it protects the community. It advises families to contact their local Party organization if they need help.**

Source G

GERMAN WOMEN!
GERMAN WOMEN!
Our Young People Defiled

The present Prussian Welfare Minister . . . has confirmed that in a German Grammar School for Girls, 63 per cent of girls had experienced sexual intercourse and 47 per cent had some form of sexual disease.This is the result of the many years during which our people, and in particular, our youth, have been exposed to a flood of muck and filth, in word and print, in the theatre and in the cinema. These are the results of the systematic Marxist [communist] destruction of the family.
Is there no possibility of salvation? Must our people, our youth, sink without hope of rescue into the muck and filth? No!!! The National Socialists must win the election so that they can put a halt to this Marxist handiwork, so that once again women are honoured and valued.

◀ **Nazi leaflet for the Reichstag elections, 1932.**

The sectoral appeal of the Nazis

Hitler found something to aim at all sections of German society.

- **The working class**. The very name of Hitler's movement, the National Socialist German Workers' Party (NSDAP) shows how important Hitler considered the working class. After all, it was the largest single sector of German people. Hitler promised to reform the economy so as to end exploitation by capitalists. He also guaranteed measures to tackle unemployment. At the same time, he made it clear that solutions to the workers' problems could be found only through the discipline of the Nazi Party, and not through trade unions and other workers' organizations.
- **The middle class**. There were really two layers in the middle class (*Mittelstand*) – what historians have called the 'old' and the 'new'. The old *Mittelstand* consisted of small-scale farmers, artisans (or skilled craftsmen) and shopkeepers. The new *Mittelstand* was composed of office workers, civil servants and teachers. Both groups feared that they would be trapped between the big capitalists on one side of them and the Communists on the other. Hitler therefore addressed a special appeal to them, promising to rescue them from their position.
- **The upper classes**. These had always despised Hitler as a vulgar upstart. Former aristocrats, estate owners and wealthy businessmen preferred the more conservative policies of the National Party (DNVP). But Hitler played skilfully upon their fears of the working class and of communism. He also stole the main policy of the DNVP, which was to end the negative impact of the Treaty of Versailles.
- **Women**. Women formed slightly over half the electorate. Many would vote according to their class connections, but Hitler aimed a special appeal on the basis of family and moral values (Sources F and G).

Who supported the Nazis?

The chart on page 35 shows how the German people changed their voting habits between 1930 and 1932. The main trend shown is obviously the increase in the support for the Nazis. Where did this support come from?

- The Centre (Z) remained fairly secure. Hitler's new following did not come from loyal Catholics, most of whom preferred the more moderate policies towards the family shown in Source H.
- The Communists (KPD) actually increased their vote. Clearly those who were already Communists were not being converted to Nazism. This is hardly surprising, since Hitler identified communism as a national enemy.
- The Social Democrats (SPD) lost support, but did not collapse. Many working-class voters did switch to the Nazis. But some also turned to the Communists, while most remained with the Social Democrats. Many workers saw through the Nazi promises and were concerned about the threat to their freedom as trade unionists.
- The Democrats (DDP) and the People's Party (DVP) had been supported almost entirely by the middle classes. By 1932 support for both had collapsed. Their votes went almost entirely to the Nazis. This was strange, since liberal people are not usually attracted to the extreme right. Yet the effect of the Depression had been so severe that the normally moderate middle classes turned into extremists.
- The National Party (DNVP) was normally supported by the upper class and part of the middle class. Many of the votes now went to the Nazis. Hitler had clearly been successful in stealing their policies. There was, however, a two-way relationship. The Nazis and the DNVP began to co-operate closely. The leader of the DNVP, **Alfred Hugenberg**, was a newspaper magnate, owning a chain of titles across Germany. In return for Nazi co-operation, he allowed Hitler to publicize Nazi policies in his newspapers. The Nazi Party was also heavily financed by business leaders and industrialists such as **Fritz Thyssen**. Hitler seemed preferable to communism and, in any case the DNVP, industrialists and the army all thought they could control Hitler and use him for their own purposes – to destroy the Republic and restore something like the previous Second Reich.

Party	May 1928	Sept 1930	July 1932	Nov 1932
Nazis (NSDAP)	12	107	230	196
National (DNVP)	73	41	37	52
People's (DVP)	45	30	7	11
Centre (Z)	62	68	75	70
Democrats (DDP)	25	20	4	2
Social Democrats (SPD)	153	143	133	121
Communists (KPD)	54	77	89	100

▲ Reichstag election results, 1928–32 (number of seats won by the main parties).

Source H

▲ An election poster from the 1920s. It reads, 'Women and men, ensure the happiness of your family and children by voting for the Christian People's Party' (Centre Party).

Source I

▲ A poster of 1932, showing what the Social Democrats believed the Nazis meant to the worker.

Source J

▶ *The real meaning of the Hitler salute,* **by the artist, John Heartfield, 1932. Heartfield, a communist, was commenting on the fact that businesses were giving money to the Nazi Party.**

Did Hitler really have the support of the German people?

Hitler was appointed Chancellor in January 1933 as the head of a coalition government in which there were only three other Nazis. This reflected the fact that the Nazi Party did not have an overall majority and therefore could not expect to govern alone. If we look at the percentage of the votes going to the Nazis up to 1932 in the chart below right, we can see that Hitler never gained much more than a third of the total votes cast.

It therefore seems that more people in 1932 opposed the Nazis than supported them. It is also quite clear that Hitler gained a large proportion of his support from the middle classes rather than from the working class. The charts on page 35 and below right show the collapse of the parties normally supported by the middle classes but the survival of the working-class parties. The middle classes also made up the majority of the actual members of the Nazi Party in 1930, as the chart below illustrates.

Party	May 1928	Sept 1930	July 1932	Nov 1932
Nazis (NSDAP)	2.6	18.3	37.4	33.1
National (DNVP)	14.2	7.0	5.9	8.8
People's (DVP)	8.7	4.5	1.2	1.9
Centre's (Z)	12.1	11.8	12.5	11.9
Democrats (DDP)	4.9	3.8	1.0	1.0
Social Democrats (SPD)	29.8	24.5	21.6	20.4
Communists (KPD)	10.6	13.1	14.3	16.9

▲ **Reichstag election results, 1928–32 (percentage of the vote received by each of the main parties).**

Category	% of Nazi Party	% of German society
Working class	28.1	45.9
Middle class of which:	66.9	35.8
White-collar workers	25.6	12.0
Self-employed	20.7	9.0
Civil servants	6.6	4.2
Small farmers	14.0	10.6

◀ **A comparison between working-class and middle-class membership of the Nazi Party in 1930.**

Source K

I have personally given altogether one million marks to the Nazi Party . . . It was during the last years preceding the Nazi seizure of power that the big industrial corporations began to make their contributions . . . and in all, the amounts given by heavy industry to the Nazis may be estimated at two million marks a year.

▲ **Fritz Thyssen, *I Paid Hitler*, 1941.**

QUESTIONS

1. Why are posters so useful for historians studying German politics between 1929 and 1933?
2. Explain the meaning of Source J. Does it present accurate information?
3. Study the chart on page 35. Why did the number of seats increase for both the right wing and the left wing parties?
4. It has been said that the Nazi Party was the only party which tried to represent the whole of Germany between 1929 and 1933. Do you agree with this? Give reasons for your answer.
5. Despite its name, the Nazi Party (NSDAP) was really a party of the middle class. Does the evidence in this section support this view?

2.5 Hitler's rise to power: a summary

1 How important was Hitler in the rise of the Nazis?

Without Hitler there could have been no Nazi movement and certainly no Nazi government in 1933. However, Hitler in turn depended on a range of factors.

- **Hitler's personal attributes** From the time he joined the DAP in 1919, Hitler emphasized the importance of strong leadership. When he displaced Drexler in 1921 he established absolute control which became known as the *Führer Prinzip*, or 'leadership principle'. This remained the case within the Party, and then within the state once he had achieved power. Hitler also gave the ideas of the Nazi Party their peculiar slant. Above all, he was responsible for their strongest single element, anti-Semitism. Hitler inspired the Party in its early years through his speeches and propaganda techniques. He also decided how the Nazis should achieve power. Before 1923 he aimed to overthrow the Republic in a *putsch*. After 1924 he switched to achieving power legally and then changing Germany afterwards.
- **Support from others** The Nazi movement may have been dominated by one man, but others contributed to its development. **Rudolf Hess**, for example, served Hitler loyally throughout the 1920s, acting as deputy Führer. He maintained Hitler's contacts with other sections of the Party while Hitler was in Landsberg Prison. Gregor Strasser and Joseph Goebbels provided the Party with its contacts in northern Germany; this was important, since Hitler's power base was in Bavaria in the south. Finally, **Ernst Röhm** was the day-to-day power behind the SA. He made sure that the 'legal' strategy did not prevent the use of violence and intimidation against opponents.
- **Objective factors** Even with his personal abilities and the support of others within the Party, Hitler could not have come to power unless other factors had worked in his favour. We can see the importance of these by comparing Hitler's success between 1929 and 1933 with his failure before 1929.

2 Why had Hitler come to power by 1933, but not by 1929?

- Germany went through a difficult period (1918–23), with economic crisis and political disturbances. But it recovered and the Stresemann era (1923–9) provided Germany with stability at home and abroad. Germany was relatively prosperous between 1923 and 1929. This was the result of the Dawes Plan which sorted out the crisis over reparations and started the flow of American investment into Germany. There was, therefore, full employment and a consumer boom.

- The moderate parties of the Weimar Republic were able to keep coalition governments going. Thus, the problems of proportional representation were not felt much before 1929. Little use was made of Article 48 of the Constitution to rule by decree and by-pass the Reichstag. Democracy was therefore upheld during this period. This meant there was very little chance for an extremist party to come to power, especially one which had experienced recent internal difficulties and the imprisonment of its leader for his part in an unsuccessful *putsch*. The vast majority of the population was not interested in Hitler's ideas and the Nazis had only a handful of seats in the Reichstag.

- Germany's stable period (1923–9) included success and consolidation at home and abroad. But this suddenly ended, so that between 1929 and 1933 crisis returned to the Republic in full force. Germany experienced a serious depression between 1929 and 1933. **The Wall Street Crash** was followed by the withdrawal of foreign investments from Germany. This caused the collapse of many businesses and a sudden increase in unemployment.

- The moderate parties of the Weimar Republic could not agree on how to deal with the problems of the depression. Coalition governments therefore broke up, and Chancellors made more and more use of Article 48. The Reichstag was by-passed and became less important. Democracy was therefore gradually replaced by dictatorship. There was now a much greater chance for an extremist party to come to power, especially one which had reorganized itself and changed its whole strategy. A larger part of the population showed interest in Hitler's ideas and policies, and Nazi policies were addressed to all classes. The result was that in July 1932, the Nazis became the largest party in the Reichstag. The politicians of 1933 therefore gave Hitler power, hoping he would use it as they wanted.

SUMMARY

The rise of Hitler

- **1914** Enlisted in German army.
- **1919** Joined the DAP.
- **1920** Placed in charge of propaganda. Helped draw up the Party Programme.
- **1921** Displaced Drexler as Party leader. Renamed the Party the NSDAP. Set up the SA.
- **1923** Attempted to seize power through the Munich *Putsch*.
- **1924–5** In Landsberg Prison. Wrote the first part of *Mein Kampf*.
- **1925** Refounded Party and adopted 'legal' strategy.
- **1926** Won over Goebbels and Strasser at the Bamberg Conference.
- **1928** The Nazis won 12 seats in the Reichstag.
- **1930** The Nazis won 107 seats in the Reichstag.
- **1932** In March Hitler lost the presidential election to Hindenburg by 19.4 million votes to 13.4 million.
- **1933** Hitler appointed Chancellor by Hindenburg on 30 January.

2.6 Exercise: Appealing to the masses

1 Read Source 3. Which other sources agree with William Shirer about the reasons why Hitler was so effective as a speaker?

2 Why did the Nazi Party organize such huge rallies?

3 'The success of the Nazi Party was more to do with Hitler than any other factor'. Using your own knowledge of the period 1925–33, do you agree or disagree with this statement?

Source 1

Fifth-formers [15-16 year-olds] are not really much concerned with the study of Hitler's thoughts; it is simply something that makes the blood pulse through one's veins and conveys an impression that something great is under way, the roaring of a stream which one does not wish to escape.

▲ **From a Protestant church report, 1931.**

Source 2

▲ **Hitler arriving to speak at a mass rally.**

Source 3

The hall was a sea of brightly coloured flags. Even Hitler's arrival was made dramatic. The band stopped playing. There was a hush over 30,000 people packed in the hall. Then the band struck up the Badenweiler March, a very catchy tune. Hitler appeared. . .strode slowly down the long centre aisle while 30,000 hands were rasied in salute. . .In such an atmosphere no wonder. . . that every word dropped by Hitler seemed like an inspired word from on high . . . every lie pronounced is accepted as high truth itself.

▲ **William Shirer, an American journalist, who watched Hitler speak in September 1934.**

Source 4

As the spirit moves him, he is promptly transformed into one of the greatest speakers of the century. Adolf Hitler enters a hall. He sniffs the air. For a minute he gropes, feels his way, senses the atmosphere. Suddenly he bursts forth. His words go like an arrow to their target, he touches each private world in the raw, liberating the mass unconscious, expressing its innermost aspirations, telling it what it most wants to hear.

▲ **Otto Strasser, a Nazi who disliked Hitler as a person, writing about his expertise as a speaker.**

Source 5

People in a crowd can sacrifice their own self-interest, personal beliefs and standards. They are easily affected by suggestions. Individuals can therefore lose their identity and become part of the mass identity.

▲ **A French psychologist in the late 19th century, explaining how people in crowds will believe things and do things they would not do on their own.**

CHAPTER 3

THE NAZI RÉGIME 1933–45

This chapter deals with the structure of the Nazi state, and the methods used to bring about the Nazi revolution. First, it defines the term 'revolution' as used for Nazi Germany. It then moves, step by step, from the creation of the Nazi dictatorship to its enforcement by terror and indoctrination, to the eventual creation of a military machine.

3.1 What was the Nazi revolution?

We have seen that after the Munich *Putsch* Hitler gave up the idea of coming to power by revolution. Instead, the Nazi revolution would take place *after* he had gained power. Between 1933 and 1934 Hitler used the powers allowed by the Constitution to convert Germany into a dictatorship. This is often called the 'legal' revolution. Once the Nazis had made sure of this, they proceeded to what Goebbels called the 'national' revolution. This made the 'legal' revolution permanent and involved the German people more fully. Together, the 'legal' and 'national' revolutions made up the Nazi revolution.

Source A

▲ **Hitler being appointed Chancellor by Hindenburg at Potsdam, 30 January 1933.**

3.2 The 'legal' revolution

Hitler was appointed Chancellor in January 1933. But Hindenburg was still Hitler's superior. Hitler was also head of a coalition government. He very much wanted to escape these constraints.

The election of March 1933

Within a few days he asked the President to dissolve the Reichstag and call an election. The election was set for 5 March 1933.

Party	Seats
Nazis (NSDAP)	288
National (DNVP)	52
Centre (Z)	74
Social Democrats (SPD)	120
Communists (KPD)	81

▲ **The results of the Reichstag election of 5 March 1933 (number of seats won).**

Source B

▲ The Reichstag building on fire, 27 February 1933.

Through this election Hitler hoped to gain an overall majority for the Nazi Party and so pass the laws he wanted. During the election campaign he persuaded President Hindenburg to declare a state of emergency under Article 48 of the Constitution. This was used to prevent the other parties, especially the Social Democrats and the Communists, from putting their ideas across properly to the German voters. Hitler's excuse was the burning of the Reichstag building which he blamed on the Communists. Some historians think that the Nazis burned the Reichstag themselves to have an excuse for declaring an emergency. Others believe it is more likely that the fire was started by a Dutch Communist, **Marinus van der Lubbe**. He denied any connection with the Communist Party, but the opportunity to accuse the Communists of trying to start a revolution was too good for the Nazis to miss.

Preparing a majority

The results of the election are shown on page 40. Although the Nazis had increased their number of seats, they still had fewer than half of them. To change the Constitution legally they needed a two-thirds majority. Hitler managed to obtain this by doing two things. First, he used the emergency decree to prevent the Communists from taking up the 81 seats they had won. Second, he won the support of the Centre Party by promising to defend the interests of the Catholic Church.

Changing the constitution

With his two-thirds majority guaranteed, Hitler was now in a position to bring about his first change to the Constitution. In March 1933 he introduced the **Enabling Act**. This made it possible for the government to introduce its own laws and to by-pass the Reichstag if it wished. In July 1933 the Enabling Act was used to introduce the **Law against the New Formation of Parties**. Germany had now officially become a one-party state – and all through the use of the Constitution.

Hitler as head of state

The one thing which Hitler still lacked was the title of President. He secured it as a result of the events of 1934.

Ernst Röhm and some other SA leaders felt that Hitler was introducing change too slowly. They began to press him to take over the **Reichswehr** (army) and merge it into the SA.

Source C

The Reichstag has passed the following law. The requirements of legal constitutional change having been met, it is being proclaimed herewith:

Article 1
In addition to the procedure outlined for the passage of legislation in the constitution, the government is also able to pass laws. . .

Article 3
The laws passed by the government shall be issued by the Chancellor and published in the official gazette.

▲ The Enabling Act, March 1933.

Source D

▲ **'They salute with both hands now'!' A cartoon by the British cartoonist, David Low, on the treatment of the SA in the Night of the Long Knives, 1934.**

Source E

The government has passed the following law, which is being proclaimed herewith:

Article 1
The sole political party existing in Germany is the National Socialist German Workers' Party.

▲ **The Law against the New Formation of Parties, July 1933.**

Source F

I swear before God to give my unconditional obedience to Adolf Hitler, Führer of the Reich and of the German people, and I pledge my word as a brave soldier to observe this oath always, even at the peril of my life.

▲ **The army's oath of allegiance to Hitler, taken from 1934 onwards.**

But Hitler feared that any attempt to do this would encourage the army to take immediate action to remove him. A far better move would be to win the support of the army so that they would support Hitler as the next President. On the night of 30 June and 1 July, therefore, Hitler used detachments of the SS to **purge** (clear out) the leaders of the SA. Altogether, several hundred SA members including Röhm, were killed in the **Night of the Long Knives**. The army was grateful and, when Hindenburg died, swore an oath of personal loyalty to Hitler. Hitler now combined the offices of Chancellor and President. From this time onwards he was known as the **Führer** (leader). His power was now complete and there was no chance of anyone else replacing him. In 1935 the Reichswehr was reorganized into the **Wehrmacht**, a new army directly under Hitler's control.

Source G

▲ **The Reichstag chamber in the early 1930s before Hitler came to power.**

Source H

▲ The Reichstag chamber in 1939.

ERNST RÖHM (1887–1934)

Born in Munich, Röhm was one of the earliest supporters of the Nazi movement and quickly became the leader of the *Sturm Abteilung* [SA]. Röhm took part in the Munich *Putsch*, but escaped imprisonment. After Hitler's rise to power he began to press hard for the takeover of the German army and considered that Hitler was too moderate. He was also resentful of the growing power being given to the SS and Heinrich Himmler. In the Night of the Long Knives, Röhm was the top target of the SS. He was taken prisoner and shot in his cell by two SS guards.

QUESTIONS

1. Explain how Hitler used the Constitution of the Weimar Republic to make Germany a dictatorship. In what ways can this be seen as a misuse of the Constitution?
2. What is the message of David Low's cartoon (Source D)?
3. If the SA was so important, why did Hitler purge the leaders?
4. Study Sources G and H. What do these two sources show about the changes that took place in the Reichstag between 1933 and 1939?

3.3 How did the Nazis enforce their political power?

The Nazis now proceeded to introduce what Goebbels called the 'national' revolution. This resulted in Germany becoming a totalitarian state. Two methods were used to control the population. The first was organized **propaganda** and **indoctrination**; the second was **terror**.

Establishing a system of propaganda and indoctrination

What is the meaning of propaganda? Strictly speaking, it comes from the word 'propagate', which means to spread. The Nazis had very specific ideas which they wanted to spread. In *Mein Kampf* Hitler set out the best way of doing this (Source A). Putting across a limited range of ideas is known as indoctrination, especially when the intention is to squeeze out other ideas.

Source A

Propaganda must confine itself to a very few points, and repeat them endlessly. Here, as with so many things in this world, persistence is the first and foremost condition of success.

▲ Adolf Hitler, *Mein Kampf*, 1925.

Source B

I view the task of the new Ministry as being to establish co-ordination between the Government and the whole people . . . It is not enough for people to be more or less reconciled to our regime, to be persuaded to adopt a neutral attitude towards us. Rather, we want to work on people until they have capitulated [given in] to us. The new Ministry has no other aim than to unite the nation behind the ideal of the national revolution.

▲ **A speech by Goebbels to a press conference, March 1933.**

Source C

▲ **A Nazi poster from the 1930s, showing the importance of radio. The slogan says 'All of Germany listens to the Führer on national radio'.**

Goebbels' ministry

The Nazis made propaganda and indoctrination a top priority. In 1933 the **Ministry for People's Enlightenment and Propaganda** was set up, under the control of Dr Joseph Goebbels. His view of its purpose is clearly seen in Source B and he intended that the lives of the entire people should be directly affected by the new body.

The Ministry was responsible for the entire organization of propaganda. Within it was a set of smaller bodies called **chambers**. One of these was the Reich Chamber of Culture. This, in turn, was subdivided into six chambers concerned with specific areas of culture: the Chamber of Archives, the Press Chamber, the Radio Chamber, the Theatre Chamber, the Music Chamber, and the Chamber of Creative Arts. To these was later added the Film Chamber.

Through these, Goebbels was able to control the whole of Germany's intellectual life and culture. He realized early on the importance of the radio as a medium for propaganda.

JOSEPH GOEBBELS (1897–1945)

Goebbels joined the Nazi Party in 1922 and was part of the 'northern' group which was won over by Hitler at the Bamberg Conference in 1926. He was appointed head of propaganda within the Party and elected to the Reichstag in 1930. Throughout the period of the Third Reich he was the Minister for Enlightenment and Propaganda. He was a brilliant speaker, with a resonant voice, and had a particular talent for presenting Nazi policies in the media, especially on radio. During the Second World War he kept the morale of the German people high through a series of famous speeches. However, he also had a vicious streak of anti-Semitism and it was he who organized the destruction of Jewish shops on Kristallnacht in 1938 [see page 55]. He remained loyal to Hitler to the end and committed suicide in April 1945, one day after the Führer.

Source D

I consider radio to be the most modern and the most crucial instrument that exists for influencing the masses. I also believe . . . that radio will, in the end, replace the press . . . First principle: At all costs avoid being boring. I put that before everything. You must help to bring forth a nationalist art and culture which is truly appropriate to the pace of modern life and to the mood of the times.

▲ **Instructions from Goebbels to the controllers of German radio, March 1933.**

The Germans owned more radios in proportion to their population than even the prosperous Americans. Goebbels was also careful to control the press, and the Press Chamber organized regular meetings with journalists to instruct them on what line to take.

The Ministry prevented the spread of 'undesirable' ideas. Universities and schools were told what to teach and there were long lists of censored books; these included most of the authors of the Weimar Republic. Libraries were ransacked and most of their contents burned by enthusiastic SA men. All academic freedom was brought to an end, an essential step in the creation of a new master race.

The use of terror

Goebbels hoped that most Germans would be won over to Nazi ideas by means of indoctrination. There were, however, bound to be many who would try to resist the new system. For them, other measures would be needed. Organizations existed to terrorize them into accepting Nazi rule. Or, as a last resort, they would remove doubters altogether.

In the next issue there must be a lead article, featured as prominently as possible, in which the decision of the Führer, no matter what it will be, will be discussed as the only correct one for Germany.

▲ **General Instruction No. 674 given to the press by the Ministry for People's Enlightenment and Propaganda.**

The SS (*Schutzstaffel*) and Gestapo

State security consisted of two main sections, which were closely related to each other. The SS was set up in 1925 as part of the SA. It was, however, more carefully disciplined than the SA, and its members wore black uniforms rather than brown. From 1929 it came under the leadership of **Heinrich Himmler** and, in 1934, it replaced the SA as the most important military group within the state. Gradually, the SS was split into three sections. One section was responsible for security. A second was the *Waffen* SS, which provided the most committed and dependable units in the armed forces. The third was the 'death's head units', which manned the concentration camps in the Second World War.

The Gestapo's full name was *Geheime Staatspolizei* (Secret State Police). It was first set up in Prussia in 1933 by **Hermann Goering**. In 1936 its control was extended to the rest of Germany and it became linked to the SS. The Gestapo was led by **Reinhard Heydrich**, who was utterly ruthless in dealing with any opposition. The purpose of the Gestapo is described in Source G. Officials were also instructed to use torture, to extract information and confessions.

Justice and the courts

In a democracy people are protected by the law against any terror imposed by officials. This had applied to the Weimar Republic. After 1933, however, the courts were '**Nazified**'.

Source F

▲ **The core of the SS. Himmler, their leader, is third from the right at the front.**

Source G

Any attempt to gain recognition for, or even uphold different ideas will be ruthlessly dealt with as the symptoms of an illness which threatens the healthy unity of the state. To discover the enemies of the state, watch them and render them harmless at the right moment is the duty of a political police.

▲ **Instructions to the Gestapo from their deputy chief, Werner Best.**

Source H

Justice is no aim in itself. It serves to maintain man's social order, an organism to which we owe culture and progress. Each and every means which serves that purpose is right. Every means which no longer does is wrong. It is not the task of justice to be mild or tough. Its task simply is to serve that purpose.

▲ **From *Hitler's Table-Talk*, 1942. This book was a record of Hitler's conversations which were noted down by his staff.**

Source I

Justice is that which is useful to the German people.

▲ **Judge Roland Freisler (1893–1945). Freisler joined the Nazi Party in 1925, and remained a loyal supporter until his death in 1945.**

Instead of justice being above politics, it became part of the Nazi state. Hitler had no time for the idea of justice being neutral. In 1934 Hitler set up the **People's Court** to try people for 'crimes' against the state. This was placed under Judge Roland Freisler, whose view of justice was even more uncompromising than Hitler's (Source I).

Punishment and concentration camps

The People's Court soon filled up with prosecutions. Between 1934 and 1939, 534 people were sentenced to death and executed for political opposition. In 1939 alone there were over 160,000 people under arrest for political offences. The SA and SS also ran a number of new prisons called concentration camps. The earliest of these was at Dachau, near Munich. Others followed including Mauthausen, Sachsenhausen, Buchenwald, Flossenbürg and Ravensbrück. These camps were filled with all types of 'undesirables', including intellectuals, dissidents, Communists, homosexuals and, of course, some Jews. Life in these camps was harsh. During the Second World War many concentration camps were turned into extermination camps (see map on page 83).

Source J

Tolerance means weakness. In the light of this conception, punishment will be mercilessly handed out whenever the interest of the fatherland warrants it.

Anyone who discusses politics, carries on controversial talks and meetings, forms cliques, loiters around with others will be hanged.

▲ **From the Regulations of Dachau Concentration Camp, 1933.**

HIMMLER AND HEYDRICH

Heinrich Himmler and Reinhard Heydrich were probably the two most feared men in Germany.

Himmler (1900–45) was given command of the SS soon after it was formed in 1929. He became really powerful after the Night of the Long Knives which destroyed many of the leaders of the SA. From that time onwards Himmler controlled the machinery of terror which included the Gestapo and the SS. He was also responsible for organizing the extermination camps in which over six million people died. He eventually committed suicide in 1945 after being captured by American troops.

Heydrich (1904–1942) was made head of the Gestapo in 1936 and was therefore Himmler's deputy. Like Himmler, he played a vital role in the extermination of the Jews. He was made Governor of Bohemia, but was assassinated in Prague in 1942 by Czech freedom fighters.

Source K

▲ **Political prisoners in Dachau concentration camp in 1933.**

3.4 What opposition was there to Nazi policies?

The Nazis seemed to impose their control over Germany with remarkable ease. Yet it would be a mistake to imagine that there was no opposition from the German people to what was happening. In this section we shall look at several groups within German society: political parties, intellectuals, young people, the Churches and officers within the army. In each case we shall consider three questions:

- In what ways did these groups offer opposition to the Nazi regime?
- What did the Nazis do to overcome this opposition?
- How successful was their opposition?

This chapter as a whole is about how the Nazis set up a system to control the people. What it was like for the various groups living within this system is dealt with in Chapter 4.

Opposition from the Social Democrats and Communists

Both the SPD and the KPD had opposed Hitler in 1932 and 1933. Social Democrat deputies turned out to the Reichstag session in March 1933 to vote against the Enabling Act. They were insulted and jostled by the SA who were assembled both inside and outside the Kroll Opera House where the Reichstag deputies were meeting. The Communists had already been prevented from taking part in the vote because they were accused by the government of having set fire to the Reichstag at the end of February. Clearly both groups were going to be a permanent nuisance to the Nazis unless something could be done about them.

The government took several measures. The two parties were banned, along with all the others, in July 1933. Both parties had had strong connections with trade unions, so, in the same year, trade unions were also banned.

Source A

▲ Forty thousand workers being presented to Hitler for inspection at a Nuremberg rally.

Source B

Whereas until 1936 the main propaganda emphasis was on distributing lots of pamphlets, at the beginning of 1936 the Communists switched to propaganda by word of mouth.
It became apparent that the Communist propaganda described above was already having some success in various factories.
In the period covered by the report, the SPD has worked mainly by means of the dissemination of news . . . and the setting up of cells in factories, sports clubs and other organizations.

▲ Extracts from a Gestapo report, commenting on the activities of Social Democrats and Communists, 1937.

A completely new way of organizing the workforce was set up. This was the **National Labour Service (RAD)** which was under the control of the Nazi Party. At the same time, the **German Labour Front (DAF)** was established which regulated working hours and disciplined workers. Responsible to the DAF were the **Beauty of Labour (SDA)** and **Strength through Joy (KDF)**. The SDA aimed to improve conditions at work. The KDF was intended to help keep the workforce happy and contented and to provide a wide range of leisure activities.

Most workers adjusted to the new arrangements and accepted that the days of bargaining for improved conditions, through trade unions, were over. But some opposition did continue. Source B shows how aware the Gestapo was that opposition from the Social Democrats and Communists had been driven underground. Secret groups were organized, which distributed anti-Nazi propaganda throughout the 1930s and well into the Second World War. On the other hand, there was a serious weakness: the two groups, which had hated each other since 1919, continued to be rivals for the support of the working class. This reduced the effectiveness of their opposition and, of course, gave the Gestapo something to work on.

Opposition from intellectuals

The Nazi régime was considered by many to be new and exciting. But a number of intellectuals and artists saw it as repressive. They felt that it was undermining the high standards in art, literature and science, to which Germany had become accustomed. It was also destroying the experiments of the Weimar Republic. Writers and artists tried to continue their work. Some spoke out against the policies of the new régime. Most avoided making any political comment and hoped that they would be left alone.

But whatever their attitude, all writers, artists and scientists were caught up in the Nazi net, cast by the chambers of the Ministry of People's Enlightenment and Propaganda.

Source C

In connection with the task, entrusted to me by the Führer, of eradicating the works of degenerate art from our museums, no fewer than 608 paintings of yours had to be seized. Many of these paintings were displayed at the exhibits of Degenerate Art in Munich, Dortmund and Berlin.
This fact could leave no doubt in your mind that your paintings did not contribute to the advancement of German culture in its responsibility toward people and nation . . .
I hereby expel you from the National Chamber of Fine Arts and forbid you any activity – professional or amateur – in the field of graphic arts.

▲ Order from The National Chamber of Fine Arts forbidding Karl Schmidt-Rottluff, a well known artist, from painting.

Source D

The much praised 'academic freedom' shall be driven out of Germany's universities.

▲ Martin Heidegger, the famous philosopher, who was at the time Rector of the University of Freiburg, May 1933.

Literature was heavily censored and most of the writers who had thrived during the Weimar Republic found themselves banned. Similarly, many artists suddenly found themselves being described as 'degenerate' and were refused permission to continue their work (Source C).

It was obviously more difficult to continue to oppose the Nazis as an artist or scientist than it was as a Social Democrat or Communist. Hence, intellectuals were left with a choice. Either they emigrated, as did **Albert Einstein**, the physicist, and most of the writers, or they stayed in Germany and adapted. **Martin Heidegger** (Source D) was one of these. He had been well known as a philosopher, but he became closely connected with Nazi ideas and politics.

Opposition from youth

Hitler laid great stress on indoctrinating the youth of Germany into the ideas of National Socialism. From the start, however, many boys – and even more girls – were not interested in the sort of regimentation which the Nazis wanted. Perhaps they were members of other youth groups or circles, possibly Catholic or Protestant. Or perhaps they pursued their own interests and did not take kindly to being organized by anyone, let alone a new system which must have seemed remote to them.

The government was well aware of all this. In 1936, therefore, it tried to tighten up with the **Law Concerning the Hitler Youth**. This was aimed especially at increasing the number of girls enrolling in the youth movement. In some ways it was remarkably successful. The Hitler Youth offered new opportunities and certainly a more exciting existence. There were, however, individuals and groups who continued to resist the pressure to join and a number of movements grew up in opposition, an example being the Edelweiss Pirates (see page 70).

Opposition from the churches

At first the Christian churches, whether Protestant or Catholic, were prepared to live with the Nazi régime. After all, it seemed to uphold more of the family and moral values than the Weimar Republic, which many Christians had considered rather corrupt.

In 1933 the Catholic Church and the Nazi government signed an agreement known as the **Concordat**, in which the Church agreed to stay out of politics if Hitler left the Catholics alone. However, the Nazis broke the agreement and interfered increasingly with Catholic liberties. The Catholic Church, therefore, broke its silence. In 1937 Pope Pius XI protested to the German Government in an **encyclical**. Then, in 1941, a letter was read from the pulpits of Catholic churches throughout Germany. This criticized the Nazi abuse of human rights and the policy of euthanasia ('mercy-killing') of the insane.

Source E

It is on youth that the future of the German nation depends. Hence it is necessary to prepare the entire German youth for its coming duties.
The government therefore has passed the following law, which is being proclaimed herewith:

Article 1
The entire German youth within the borders of the Reich is organized in the Hitler Youth.

Article 2
It is not only in home and school, but in the Hitler Youth as well, that all of Germany's youth is to be educated, physically, mentally, and morally, in the spirit of National Socialism, to serve the nation and the racial community.

▲ **From the Law Concerning the Hitler Youth, 1 December 1936.**

▼ **A poster by Ludwig Hohlwin, advertising the League of German Maidens in the Hitler Youth.**

Source F

The Protestants went through similar stages. At first there was co-operation and the Nazis displayed banners in many of their churches. Then the Government attempted to set up the Reich Church, with a strongly Nazified structure. Protestant leaders throughout Germany were opposed to this (Source H). Many Christians, both Protestant and Catholic, opposed the Nazis in many ways (see Chapter 5).

Towards the end of the 1930s the Nazis attempted to replace Christianity altogether. They introduced a **Faith Movement**, which was based on pagan ideas and festivals. But this had virtually no effect in the longer term.

Source G

▲ **Nazi banners in a Protestant church in Berlin, 1934.**

Opposition from within the army

Most of the officers and men within the armed forces swore the oath of allegiance to Hitler in 1934. Some, however, remained highly suspicious of the Nazis. A few, like General Ludwig Beck (Chief of the General Staff), secretly tried to encourage Britain and France to resist Hitler's ambitions abroad.

Hitler introduced three measures to ensure the total obedience of the army's high command. First, he Nazified it, insisting that Nazi insignia should be added to military uniforms. Second, he placed the *Waffen* SS at its head, ensuring that they would always be in control of the most important operations. Third, in 1938, he retired or sacked large numbers of generals and set up a new army high command, the *Oberkommando Wehrmacht* (OKW). From this time onwards Hitler was responsible for all military decisions. This did not, however, prevent the eventual return of opposition (see Chapter 5).

Source H

We declare that the constitution of the German Evangelical [Protestant] Church has been destroyed. Its legally constituted organs no longer exist. The men who have seized the church leadership have divorced themselves from the Christian Church.

▲ **A statement by the Confessional Church condemning those Protestants who co-operated with the Nazis.**

QUESTIONS

1. **a** Which groups opposed the Nazis and why?
   b How did the Nazis react?
2. Which form of opposition was the most dangerous to the Nazis? Give your reasons.

Conclusion

During peacetime the Nazi government was able to take measures against various forms of opposition. These were not totally successful and historians are now pointing out some of their shortcomings. Nevertheless, they did keep the lid firmly down. Although dissent continued, it did relatively little damage to the régime, largely because there was no unity of organization or purpose. The same applied during the first phase of the Second World War between 1939 and 1941, when all went well for Germany. We shall see in Chapter 5, however, that the second phase of the War brought all the various strands of opposition together and posed a more serious threat to Hitler.

3.5 How did the Nazis build the racial state?

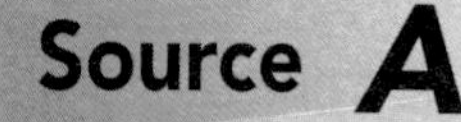

Source A

Our nation's only true possession is its good blood.

▲ **Walther Darré, Reich Food Minister in 1933. Darré wrote numerous books about racial policy.**

Source B

The first principle for us was and is the recognition of the values of blood and selection.
We went about it like a seedsman who, wanting to improve the strain of a good variety which has become crossbred and lost its vigour, goes through the fields to pick the seeds of the best plants. We sorted out the people who we thought unsuitable for the formation of the SS simply on the basis of outward appearance.

▲ **A speech by Heinrich Himmler, head of the SS, 12 November 1935.**

Source C

◀ **A Nazi poster of 1938 showing the ideal Aryan family.**

In Chapter 2 we looked at the basic ideas spread by the Nazis before Hitler came to power. The most important of these concerned race and anti-Semitism. The first aimed to create an **Aryan** master race within Germany, the second to destroy Jewish influences. Once the Nazis had achieved power, the racial policies were given absolute priority. They were the central focus of the Nazi revolution.

Making the master race

Mussolini, the fascist dictator of Italy, believed that the nation was the greatest of human achievements. For Hitler, the nation was only the first step towards something higher still: the Aryan or master race. Although Hitler believed the German people were of Aryan descent, he felt that they needed to be purified by a programme of selective breeding. They would also have to be indoctrinated into accepting their new role.

Selective breeding

The programme of purifying the German people was entrusted to the SS, which became much more than a mere security service. It recruited its members only from men with the correct Aryan physical appearance. That is, they were tall, with fair hair and blue or grey eyes. They were allowed to marry only after the racial pedigree of their future wives had been checked. The purpose of all this is explained in Source B. The SS also had a network of race farms throughout Germany. Women who had been approved by the authorities were brought to these farms. Their purpose was to breed children fathered by SS officers. Through programmes like this, the Nazis believed, the Aryan race would be purified.

Source D

▲ **Children being examined for suitable Aryan racial characteristics.**

Source E

The eternal God created for our nation a law that is peculiar to its own kind. It took shape in the leader, Adolf Hitler, and in the National Socialist state created by him.

This law speaks to us from the history of our people, a history grown of blood and soil.

▲ **An outline of beliefs of a German Christian group.**

Racial indoctrination

The Nazi régime brought race into everything. Race studies and **eugenics** were taught in schools and universities. Eugenics looks at the ways of controlling reproduction in humans, so that only those people who have 'correct' or desirable characteristics are allowed to breed. Scientists were ordered to promote racial studies not only in Biology but also in Physics and Chemistry. Those who protested that this destroyed the whole purpose of scientific investigation were forced to stop practising. Even religion became a target. The Nazis tried to show that there were really two strands in the Old Testament. One was Jewish, the other Aryan. They tried to convince people that God had a special purpose for the Aryan people and Hitler played a key part in this (Source E). New paintings and sculptures were produced to show the German people their racial heritage and their racial future; these are dealt with in Chapter 4.

The building of a master race was the purpose of the Nazi revolution. But the logical result of this was violence. This took two forms. The first was the conquest of 'inferior' races outside Germany (see Chapter 5). The other was the persecution of 'inferior' races within Germany, especially the Jews (Source F).

▼ **The Nazis organized a boycott of Jewish shops on 1 April 1933. The sign reads: 'Germans! Protect yourselves! Do not buy from Jews!' This SA man is making sure nobody enters this shop which is owned by a Jew.**

Source F

Persecuting the Jews

The Nazis began to persecute the Jews as soon as Hitler came to power. Their anti-Semitic policies went through three quite distinct stages.

Stage 1 The denial of civil rights 1933–8

For the first five years the Nazis gradually deprived the Jews of their rights as German citizens. From the start they refused them the protection of the police and, on 1 April 1933, SA men organized a boycott of Jewish shops (see Source F on page 53). In April 1933 Jewish civil servants were dismissed, although President Hindenburg insisted that this should not apply to those who had served in the First World War. In September 1933 Jews were banned from inheriting land.

The year 1935 produced a rush of laws, probably because the restraining hand of President Hindenburg was no longer there. Parks, swimming baths, restaurants and public buildings were all closed to Jews. In the same year, the **Nuremberg Laws** (or the Laws for the Protection of German Blood and German Honour) made illegal any marriage or sexual intercourse between Germans and Jews.

Throughout this period hatred for Jews was deliberately spread by **Julius Streicher** in his newspaper, *Der Stürmer*. This contained vicious lies of the type shown in Source G. In schools, meanwhile, Jewish children were humiliated in front of their class.

Source G

The blood of the victims is to be forcibly tapped ... the fresh [or powdered] blood of the slaughtered child is further used by young married Jewish couples, by pregnant Jewesses, for circumcision and so forth.

▲ **From the anti-Jewish newspaper, *Der Stürmer*.**

Source H

Paragraph 1
Marriages between Jews and Citizens of German or kindred blood are hereby forbidden. Marriages performed despite this ban are void.

Paragraph 2
Extramarital intercourse between Jews and citizens of German or kindred blood is forbidden.

▲ **Extracts from the Laws for the Protection of German Blood and German Honour, 1935.**

Source I

▶ **Jewish schoolchildren being humiliated in front of their class.**

Stage 2 The acceleration of persecution 1938–41

From 1938 onwards the position of the Jews in Germany deteriorated rapidly. There were several reasons for this. First, the Nazi régime was much more in control than it had been in the early 1930s. Second, indoctrination and terror were removing possible opposition. And third, Hitler had scored a number of successes abroad in 1938, including the annexation of Austria. The Nazis knew that there would be no pressure to change their policies from Britain and France.

The turning point came with a night of violence against Jews on 9 November 1938. Throughout Germany, Jewish shops and synagogues were ransacked or destroyed and many people were killed or injured. The event was named ***Kristallnacht*** ('Crystal Night') after the broken glass which littered streets everywhere. It was probably organized in advance by the SA, acting under orders from Goebbels. Officially, however, Goebbels claimed that the violence was the result of the 'righteous indignation' of the German people against those who were swindling them.

After 1938 the Jews lost their last remaining liberties. They were no longer allowed to trade and they were even deprived of the right to choose their children's names: they now had to keep to an approved list. In 1941 they were forced to wear a large, yellow six pointed star sewn on to their coats, and they were segregated into ghettoes. The extent to which the hatred of Jews had intensified can be seen in the illustration from a children's book, shown in Source J.

Stage 3 The Holocaust 1941–5

Before 1941 there was no scheme for the **genocide**, or mass destruction of the Jewish people. This was introduced during the Second World War and is known as the Holocaust. It will be dealt with on pages 83–6.

QUESTIONS

1. Describe what is happening in Source J.
2. Why is this cartoon an example of Nazi propaganda against the Jews?
3. 'The Jews were as badly off in Nazi Germany in 1933 as they were in 1941.' Does the evidence in this chapter support this view? Explain your answer.

Source J

▲ **Anti-Semitic cartoon from a children's book, 1938.**

3.6 How did the Nazis rebuild German culture?

The racial state was the main target of the Nazi revolution. The purpose of culture was to present the image of this to the German people. This applied especially to the visual arts – to painting, sculpture and architecture.

Nazi art

As we have already seen, the National Chamber of Fine Arts condemned many works produced during the Weimar Republic as 'decadent'. An example would have been Paul Klee's picture, *Dancing with Fear*. Others would have been the works of Ernst Barlach, Max Beckman and Oskar Kokoschka.The work of these artists and many others was shown to the public in special exhibitions of 'degenerate art'. Why did the Nazis object so much to these works? Hitler felt that art must serve the state, whereas the artists of the Weimar Republic had believed in 'art for art's sake'. The Nazis considered that such paintings and sculptures undermined racial purity. They also despised them because they were experimental and did not show human beings in a realistic way.

Source A

▲ ***Dancing with Fear*, painted by Paul Klee in 1938.**

Instead, the painters and sculptors of the Third Reich produced works which were designed to show Germans in the way that the racial state demanded. The best known Nazi artists were Ivo Saliger, Arthur Kampf and Adolf Ziegler (who was also President of the Chamber of Fine Arts). Their favourite medium was myths and legends.

One painting, *Venus and Adonis* by Kampf, is worth looking at in some detail (Source B). This was one of the most famous paintings of the Nazi period. Like many others, it showed a classical theme but the message was updated to fit into the new Aryan image. As a piece of propaganda it effectively illustrates all the key Nazi ideas. Both figures are healthy, strong and vigorous. The man is armed, alert and ready to fight; behind him is a horse, the symbol of war. The woman is submissive and totally dependent on the man's protection. At another level, we might interpret the man as the SS and the woman as Germany. Either way, the emphasis is on strength and victory.

But how good is it as a piece of art? Two points can be made. The first is that the brushwork is very basic and natural details, such as the tree and leaves are badly painted. More important, however, is the fault in the composition. The whole painting consists of sections copied from the masters of the past.

The woman is an almost exact replica of a 16th century picture by Titian (Source C). The horse is lifted from a painting by David (Source D). And the man's head bears more than a passing resemblance to Michelangelo's fresco (Source E). This much prized treasure of the new art was therefore a forgery. The *real* examples of 'new art' were the paintings in the museums of degenerate art!

Source B

◀ *Venus and Adonis*, painted by Arthur Kampf in 1939.

Source C

◀ *Venus and Adonis* by Titian (1487–1576).

Source D

▼ *Napoleon crossing the Alps* by Jacques-Louis David (1748–1825).

Source E

▼ *The Creation of Adam* by Michelangelo (1475–1564).

Source F

▲ **Architect's model of the People's Hall, Berlin.**

Nazi architecture

Hitler had always had a particular interest in architecture and he probably would have practised this as a career had he been accepted by the Vienna Academy of Fine Arts. Instead, as a dictator, he used it to give his régime the appearance of power and permanence. He proposed to put up buildings which would, like the Third Reich itself, last for a thousand years. He discussed his ideas with his chief architect and Minister of Armaments, **Albert Speer**.

The focal point of their plans was the rebuilding of Berlin. This was due to be completed by 1950, when the name of the capital would be changed to **Germania**. The whole of the city centre would be knocked down and replaced by huge buildings, monuments and two great highways which would run from east to west and north to south. Where they met there would be a central square on which would stand the People's Hall.

This would be able to accommodate 150,000 people and would be over 300 metres high – easily the largest domed structure in the world.

Most of these plans went no further than the model stage. But Hitler was so committed to them that he was still dreaming of the new Berlin while the old one was being destroyed by the Russians in 1945. There are, however, a few completed buildings which can be seen today.

Nazi films

A newer medium than painting was the cinema. Goebbels and Hitler made use of this in several ways.

Source G

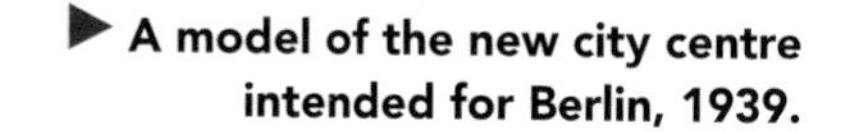

► **A model of the new city centre intended for Berlin, 1939.**

A brilliant film actress and director, **Leni Riefenstahl**, was commissioned to make a detailed record of mass rallies, festivals, speeches and the 1936 Olympic Games. The results were probably the most impressive propaganda films ever made, one of which was ***Triumph of the Will***. These films were shown in cinemas throughout Germany to remind the people of the scale of the changes which were taking place, and to encourage everyone to take part in them. Stills from this film provide most of the photographs used today to illustrate key events in the Third Reich. Examples are shown in Sources H and I.

Films were also used to put across racial values and ideas. The principles of eugenics and racial breeding were explained by drawing comparisons with crops and animals. Above all, the cinema became a powerful weapon in stirring up hatred against Jewish people in Germany.

Source H

▲ A religious procession organized by the National Reich Church. A still from the propaganda film, *Triumph of the Will*.

▼ A small section of a mass rally showing the huge numbers attending. A still from the propaganda film, *Triumph of the Will*.

Source I

SUMMARY

1933

- Reichstag Fire.
- Enabling Act.
- Law against the New Formation of Parties.
- Ministry for People's Enlightenment and Propaganda set up.
- Gestapo set up in Prussia.
- First concentration camps set up.
- National Labour Service (RAD) set up.

1934

- Night of the Long Knives.
- Hitler became Führer

1935

- Nuremberg Laws passed.

1936

- Gestapo merged with SS.
- Hitler Youth set up.

1938

- *Kristallnacht*.

QUESTIONS

1. In what ways did the Nazis consider art, architecture and films important?
2. Why do you think Hitler ordered 'degenerate art' to be shown to the public, rather than to be destroyed?
3. Why did Hitler want to rebuild Berlin?

3.7 How did Hitler change the German economy?

When Hitler came to power in 1933, he had two main economic priorities. One was to pull Germany through the Great Depression and greatly reduce unemployment. The other was to change the whole economic base, so that Germany could rearm and once again become the greatest military power in Europe.

Schacht and the period 1933–5

During the first three years of Nazi rule the economy was directed by the President of the Reichsbank, **Hjalmar Schacht**. He believed in a steady expansion of trade and a strict control on the amount of money spent on **rearmament**. Schacht promoted trade agreements between Germany and less developed countries. By these Germany would import raw materials which would be paid for by German industrial goods. In his **New Plan** of 1934 Schacht also tried to reduce imports into Germany and to strengthen the currency. These policies were designed to rebuild Germany's prosperity, and Schacht insisted that faster rearmament would only interfere. Hitler soon became impatient with Schacht's caution.

Hitler's ideas about rearmament

In fact, Hitler had a very different strategy. He felt that it was possible to convert Germany into a war machine. This could be done through the method of ***Blitzkrieg***. This literally meant 'lightning war'. Germany would conquer other countries one by one by means of a rapid attack. It would then absorb the economy of the defeated country and, strengthened, would go on to the next. In this way Germany would expand steadily and achieve the ***Lebensraum*** (living space) that Hitler wanted. *Blitzkrieg* had the advantage of not needing too many sacrifices from the German people. Certainly their working hours would have to increase and their wages would need to be held steady. There might even be fewer consumer goods to buy than in Britain. Nevertheless, it would be possible both to maintain a reasonable standard of living and, at the same time, to prepare for war.

Source A

▲ **An armaments factory in Düsseldorf in 1939.**

Source B

The extent of the military development of our resources cannot be too large, nor its pace too swift. If we do not succeed in bringing the German army as rapidly as possible to the rank of premier army in the world, then Germany will be lost!

I thus set the following tasks:

i The German armed forces must be operational within four years.
ii The German economy must be fit for war within four years.

▲ **From Hitler's memorandum on the Four Year Plan, 1936.**

This is why *Blitzkrieg* seemed to be the perfect solution, offering the prospect of eventual wealth through conquest, while avoiding all the suffering that Stalin's Five Year Plans were bringing to the Russian people.

Goering and the Four Year Plan 1936–40

In 1936 Hitler put this strategy into operation. He issued a secret memorandum introducing a **Four Year Plan** (Source B). This Plan was designed to speed up rearmament and prepare Germany for war within four years. It was also intended to make Germany self-sufficient in raw materials through the development of home-produced substitutes: this process was known as '**autarchy**'. In 1936 Schacht was dismissed and Goering took over the implementation of the Four Year Plan.

The result of this change

The Four Year Plan brought a considerable increase in the expenditure on armaments and in the size of the German army. This led to growing confidence in Hitler's foreign policy and his open defiance of the Treaty of Versailles. He remilitarized the Rhineland in 1936, annexed Austria in the ***Anschluss*** of 1938 and took over the Sudetenland of Czechoslovakia in 1938. In March 1939 Germany absorbed Bohemia and then made demands of Poland. Hitler ignored the guarantee made to Poland by Britain and France, and invaded Poland in September 1939. This brought about a major conflict, as both Britain and France declared war on Germany. The consequences of this are dealt with in detail in Chapter 5.

Source C

1933	1.9	**1938**	18.4
1936	5.8	**1939**	32.3

▲ **Total military expenditure of the German government 1933–9 (in billions of marks).**

Source D

Number of battalions in:

	1933	1936	1939
Infantry	84	334	906
Artillery	24	148	482
Tank	0	16	34

▲ **The increase in the size of the German army, 1933–9.**

QUESTIONS

1. How important were Schacht and Goering in the moves to rearm Germany?
2. *Blitzkrieg* means 'lightning war'. It has been said that this is as much an economic term as a military one. Why?

HERMAN GOERING (1893–1946)

Goering was a member of the aristocracy and had a distinguished record as a fighter pilot during the First World War. He joined the Nazi Party during the 1920s and became a politician of national repute. In 1932 he was elected speaker of the Reichstag and then made its president in 1933. He was one of the three Nazis in Hitler's government, formed at the end of January 1933. He was largely responsible for persuading President Hindenburg to allow the use of Article 48 of the Constitution to undermine the other parties in the general election campaign of 1933. As Prime Minister of Prussia, he also set up the Gestapo together with the first of the concentration camps. He defied the terms of the Treaty of Versailles and set up the Luftwaffe, or German airforce, in 1933. He also took over the direction of the economy from Schacht and was responsible for implementing the Four Year Plan between 1936 and 1940. In recognition of his achievements, Hitler made Goering Reichsmarshal in 1940. During the Second World War, however, Goering was blamed by Hitler for the failure of Germany to defeat Britain. Goering was captured by the Allies in 1945 and sentenced to death at the war crimes tribunal at Nuremberg in 1946. He escaped the hangman, however, by taking cyanide on the night of his execution.

3.8 Exercise: The Berlin Olympics 1936

1 Read Source 2. Why might the Nazis have halted the persecution of the Jews during the Olympic Games?

2 Study Sources 1, 4 and 5. Hitler, as Head of State of the host nation, shook hands with most gold medal winners, but he refused to shake hands with Jesse Owens. What would the German spectators have thought of this?

3 In what ways did the Nazi régime encourage men, women and children to lead healthy lives?

4 Were the Germans in 1936 'a happy, friendly people united under Hitler'? Use your knowledge about Nazi Germany to support your answer.

Source 1

▶ **An official poster for the Olympic Games held in Berlin, 1936.**

Source 2

The Olympic Games were held in Berlin in August 1936. The signs 'Jews not welcome' were quietly taken down from shops and hotels, the persecution of the Jews halted for a time and the country put on its best behaviour. No earlier games had seen such organization, nor such a lavish display of entertainment. The visitors, especially those from England and America, were greatly impressed by what they saw – a happy, friendly people united under Hitler.

▲ **From a history of Nazi Germany written in the USA in 1959.**

Source 3

The people's state must organize its educational work in such a way that the bodies of the young are trained from infancy onwards, so as to be tempered and hardened for the demands made on them in later years. Not a day should be allowed in which the young pupil does not have one hour of physical training in the morning and one in the evening.

▲ **Hitler wrote down his views about the importance of physical education in *Mein Kampf*, first published in 1925.**

Source 4

▲ **The famous black athlete, Jesse Owens of the USA, winning the men's 100 metres final at the Berlin Olympics. He won three individual gold medals and one team gold (for the 4 by 100 metres relay).**

Source 5

The athletic events of the Olympic Games at Berlin ended on August 9. By then most of the Olympic records had been beaten and a number of new world records had been set up. There was no doubt that Jesse Owens, the American negro, had put up the most wonderful of many performances. Others of America's negro team, notably Metcalfe and Woodruff, also covered themselves with glory.

▲ **A report from the *Illustrated London News*, August 1936.**

CHAPTER 4

LIFE IN THE THIRD REICH

4.1 Did the people benefit from Nazi economic policies?

When the Nazis came to power in 1933 they promised all sections of the population a better deal from the economy. This is one of the main reasons why the middle classes had supported Hitler. They had been so badly affected by the Great Depression that they believed Hitler's promise that the Nazis would restore their prosperity, and their place in society. Many members of the working class also believed that Hitler would deal with the basic problem of unemployment.

Was the faith of these people in the Nazis justified? This section looks at some of the evidence. A lecturer from Cambridge University, who visited Germany in 1938, gave his view in Source A. This is a good starting point to assess Nazi economic policies since it makes a key observation: things were improving, but not as much as they might have done.

Source A

No one who is acquainted with German conditions would suggest that the standard of living is a high one, but the important thing is that it has been rising in recent years.

▲ **The view of a Cambridge University economics lecturer in 1938.**

Wages as an indicator of prosperity: the evidence of statistics

On the surface it seems that the German workforce did benefit from Nazi policies. Unemployment fell quickly after 1933 by comparison with the high levels seen in the last years of the Weimar Republic (Source B).

Source B

Unemployed in Germany (in millions)

Year	Unemployed	Year	Unemployed
1928	1.8	1935	2.2
1932	6.0	1936	1.6
1933	4.8	1937	0.9
1934	2.7	1938	0.5

Closer analysis, however, reveals some of the truth behind these figures. In fact, unemployment levels declined everywhere, including Britain and the USA as the world came out of depression. German workers were not necessarily better off than they would have been under a non-Nazi Government. It is true that unemployment reached a lower level in Germany than in Britain, but this could be readily explained by the use of compulsory labour on public works projects such as the construction of houses, waterways and **autobahns**.

What about wage levels? (Source C). During periods of high unemployment wages can be expected to stand still or go down.

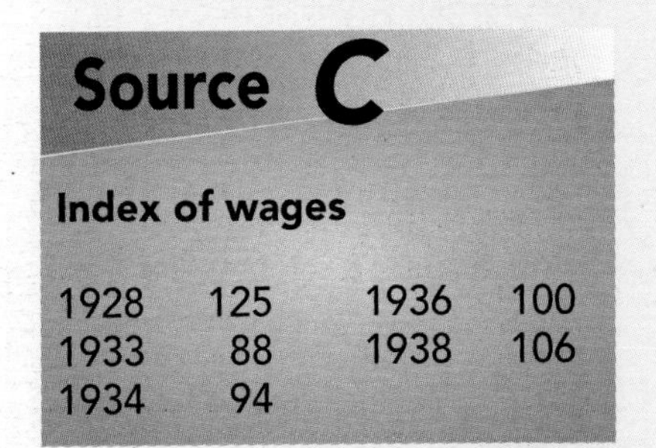

Source C

Index of wages

Year	Index	Year	Index
1928	125	1936	100
1933	88	1938	106
1934	94		

▲ **The term 'index' means that the wages in one year, in this case 1936, are taken to be 100. The other years are measured against this.**

Source D

National income
(in billions of marks)

1928	72	1936	64
1932	43	1938	80
1933	44		

Source E

Wages as a percentage of national income

1928	62	1934	62
1932	64	1936	59
1933	63	1938	57

Source F

[The workers] compared the conditions of life in the Third Reich with the abnormally low standard of living in 1932 and not with the more representative one of 1929. By raising living standards a few points above subsistence level the Nazis thus appeared to improved things drastically, even though the standard of living was well below what had been taken for granted in the late 1920s.

▲ **An extract from Richard Grunberger, *A Social History of the Third Reich*, 1971.**

Source G

Index of industrial and consumer goods

Industrial		*Consumer*
100	1928	100
56	1933	80
81	1934	91
114	1936	100
144	1938	116

This is what happened between 1929 and 1933, the worst years of the Depression. Then, as economic recovery took place, wages began to increase (Source C). This seems to show that the Nazi régime translated recovery directly into greater prosperity for the people.

Or does it? Wages were still lower in 1938 than they had been in 1928. Source D, however, shows that Germany's national income (the total value of goods produced) was actually higher in 1938.

This means that wages rose more slowly than production in Nazi Germany. This is confirmed by Source E, which shows a steady decline in wages as a percentage of national income. In other words, the workforce was putting more into the economy than they were getting out of it. People worked longer hours for their wages. The length of the working day had increased by an average of 10% by 1939 in comparison with 1928. Most people worked 49 hours per week. This rose to 52 by 1943 and then shot up to over 60. These last two figures, however, reflect the special conditions of wartime. The figures were always disguised by the authorities, who stressed how fortunate people were to have jobs.

Other indicators of prosperity

Another way of assessing whether people were better off under the Nazis is to find out whether what they were producing benefited them personally. We can do this by comparing the manufacture of **industrial goods** (machinery and armaments) with **consumer goods** (items for household and personal use). If these are indexed at the same level in 1928, we can see that the workforce in Nazi Germany produced industrial goods at a much faster rate than consumer goods (Source G).

The Government made this official policy for two reasons. One was that it aimed to increase Germany's military strength and prepare for war. The other was to control the number of consumer goods available. This would mean that the workforce would have less to spend their money on and would therefore appear to be reasonably well-off.

The Nazis had never promised a capitalist or free-enterprise society. They had always made it clear that the Government would control the economy for the benefit of the people as a whole. So perhaps it would have been unreasonable to have expected a sudden rush of prosperity for individuals and particular classes. But, if wages did not go up in proportion to the national income, did the German people benefit, perhaps, in other ways?

The workforce

The Nazi Government claimed that its policies were of immense benefit to the workers. It set up two movements to care directly for the workers' interests. The **Beauty of Labour** (*Schonheit der Arbeit* or SDA) aimed to improve conditions at work, such as cleanliness, lighting and noise levels; it also provided hot meals in the workplace. The justification for keeping wages down was that the extra benefits at work would be a good substitute. The **Strength through Joy** movement (*Kraft durch Freude* or KDF) was designed to keep the workforce happy by filling people's leisure time with a wide variety of activities which took place outside working time. The most productive and loyal workers could even qualify for a cruise on a KDF liner. Throughout the 1930s the German workers were constantly told that they were better off than their fellow workers in the Soviet Union (which was true) and in Britain (which was not).

There were, however, disadvantages for the workers. These two organizations replaced the former trade unions, which had been responsible for negotiating conditions of work and wages with the industrialists. Under the new system there was no one to put the point of view of the workforce. The owners of the great industries, especially steel and armaments, were given preferential treatment by the Nazi Government, whose priority was to gear Germany for war in the shortest possible time. It is therefore not surprising that some workers, especially those who were Social Democrats and Communists, secretly tried to tell the others that the Government was exploiting them. It had frozen their wages, increased their working hours and made it impossible to complain about conditions. And in return the workers were obliged to take on extra activities in their own time.

Source H

▲ A Strength through Joy (KDF) poster of 1938, advertising cruises for the German workforce.

Source I

Concerts, popular entertainments, operas, operettas, theatre, variety cabaret, evening variety shows, films, exhibitions, guided tours, basic [sporting] course, special gymnastics, light athletics, swimming, boxing, wrestling, games, water sports, winter sports, special sports, factory sports, vacation journeys, short trips, cruises, hikes.

▶ Leisure activities organized by Strength through Joy (KDF).

Source J

▲ **A 1938 poster promoting the *Volkswagen*, or people's car. It tells people to save five marks per week to buy their own car.**

Source K

▲ **A poster advertising the German autobahns.**

The Government did try to persuade the people that they were more affluent by developing a new consumer product. This was the *Volkswagen*, or 'people's car'.

There were also advertisements showing the new autobahns, designed to provide the best possible motoring conditions. Source K shows one of these posters. Between 1933 and 1938 the Nazi Government built almost 2,000 miles of autobahns.

Most people, however, never received their car – either because they never managed to save enough or because the *Volkswagen* was not made in sufficient numbers. Production figures were less than half of those of the car industry in Britain, even though the British industrial economy as a whole was smaller than Germany's. As for the autobahns: these were built mainly for military purposes, to allow the quick movement of soldiers in wartime.

QUESTIONS

1. Do Sources B to G (pages 63–4) support the statement made in Source A (page 63)? Give reasons for your answer.
2. Did the German workforce lose more than they gained from the ending of trade unions? Explain your answer.

4.2 What was it like to be young in Nazi Germany?

At first, most children would have been influenced in their views of Hitler by their parents. Since Hitler received less than half the vote in March 1933, we can reasonably assume that over half of Germany's youth up to that point received negative ideas about the Nazis. Did their views change?

Education

Numerous photographs exist of Hitler with children. Source A is typical of his efforts to identify with youth and to show his popularity with this age group.

Young people were constantly exposed to Hitler's ideas through the school system. The whole purpose of education was turned upside down. Instead of opening minds, it was designed to close them, as Source B shows.

Source A

◀ Hitler shown with children.

The content of the school curriculum was slanted very much to what the Nazis saw as the main needs: military skills for boys and domestic skills for girls.

All subjects were used as a vehicle for Nazi ideas. Even mathematics could be used to encourage an acceptance of the killing of the insane (Source D).

Source B

The whole purpose of education is to create Nazis.

▲ **Said by the Nazi Minister of Education, Bernhard Rust.**

Source C

German Language, History, Geography, Chemistry and Mathematics must concentrate on military subjects – the glorification of military service and of German heroes.

▲ **From an official statement on the purpose of education for boys.**

Source D

The construction of a lunatic asylum costs 6 million marks. How many houses at 15,000 marks each could have been built for that amount?

▲ **A problem from a mathematics textbook of the late 1930s.**

Source E

◀ A Hitler Youth camp at Nuremberg in 1934.

Source F

▲ A fund-raising poster for the Hitler Youth.

How popular would all this have been? Many pupils would have preferred it to the previous system of more academic studies. They would also have been attracted by the emphasis given to sport. But what of the large numbers of young people who would have thrived on academic courses? They must have felt frustrated intellectually, and possibly resentful at having to spend so much of their time on outside activities. Girls, in particular, had reason to feel that their education was being downgraded and that they were being forced into a domestic role. Many may have wanted this, but some would have been profoundly unhappy about it.

The Hitler Youth

Membership of the Hitler Youth was made compulsory in 1936. It consisted of a variety of levels. Boys from 6 to 10 joined the *Pimpf* (Little Fellows) and were involved in activities such as hiking and camping. At 10 they took a test (or *Pimpfenprobe*) to enable them to move into the *Deutsche Jungvolk* (German Young People), where they learned more about Nazi ideology and military matters. Between the ages of 14 and 18 they were enrolled in the Hitler *Jugend* (Hitler Youth), which had a much stronger emphasis on military discipline and training. Girls, meanwhile, joined the *Jungmädel* (Young Maidens) to the age of 14 and were taught how to care for their health and prepare for motherhood.

Source G

Year	Number of 10–18 year-olds in Hitler Youth (boys and girls)	Total number of 10–18 year-olds in the population
1933	2.3	7.5
1934	3.6	7.7
1935	3.9	8.2
1936	5.4	8.7
1937	5.9	9.1
1938	7.0	9.1
1939	7.3	8.9

▲ Membership of the Hitler Youth, 1933–9 (figures in millions).

Source H

We had to be present at every public meeting and at youth rallies and sports. The weekends were crammed full with outings, campings and marches. It was all fun in a way, and we certainly got plenty of exercise, but it had a bad effect on our school reports. We had no time for homework.

◀ **A description of the League of German Maidens, by a former member.**

From 14 to 21 girls belonged to the *Bund Deutscher Mädel* (League of German Maidens).

The activities at all levels were put across in propaganda films as being enormously popular. Riefenstahl's film, *Triumph of the Will* contains several scenes showing the fun of life in a youth camp, as well as the sheer scale of the numbers involved (Source E). Happy and dedicated Aryan faces were also shown on money-raising posters (Source F). It is obviously difficult to assess the extent to which the Hitler Youth really did appeal. We know that the numbers in the movement gradually increased, but the recollections of former members contain very mixed feelings (Sources H and I).

Source I

When I became a leader in the *Jungvolk* the negative aspects became very obvious. I found the compulsion and the requirement of absolute obedience unpleasant. I appreciated that there must be order and discipline in such a large group of boys, but it was exaggerated.

▶ **A description of the *Jungvolk* by a former leader.**

Alternative youth organizations

We should not suppose that all of Germany's youth accepted being organized or regimented. The Nazis succeeded in killing off other official youth organizations, such as those which had once been attached to the SPD. In the late 1930s, and during the period of the Second World War, however, several entirely new youth groups developed in Germany. Their members were rebellious and behaved in ways which the Nazi officials saw as a real threat.

Some groups cultivated appearances which went directly against what was considered acceptable. They grew their hair long and also became involved in jazz music from the USA and Britain. Source J shows two such 'swingers'. Others imitated characteristics from abroad, especially England, which were calculated to annoy the authorities most (Source K).

Source J

▲ **Two 'swing types' from a book on youth criminality, published in Germany in 1941.**

Source K

▲ **An 'English casual' from the same book as above.**

Source L

◀ Edelweiss Pirates being publicly hanged in Cologne in 1944.

Source M

Every child knows who the Kittelbach Pirates are. They are everywhere; there are more of them than there are Hitler Youth . . . They don't agree with anything. They don't go to work either; they're always down by the canal, at the lock.

▲ The complaint of a mining instructor from Oberhausen, 1941.

The real problem, however, came with the groups which were really gangs. Three examples were the **Navajos Gang**, the **Kittelbach Pirates** and, above all, the **Edelweiss Pirates**.

The police received constant streams of complaints from outraged local residents, especially in the Cologne area.

The favourite activity of these groups was to ambush and beat up Hitler Youth patrols, although this is something that the Nazi authorities were not too anxious to publicize. During the Second World War, Edelweiss Pirates collected propaganda dropped from Allied aircraft and pushed it through letterboxes. They were also known to help Allied airmen escape. Some even went so far as to join political resistance movements. Whenever they could, the Gestapo made examples of gang members, as Source L shows.

Source N

▲ Members of the Navajos, a Cologne based gang,1940.

Conclusion

The Nazis mainly succeeded in replacing the earlier forms of youth organizations which had once flourished in Germany. They set up the Hitler Youth, an organization which many – perhaps the majority – found new and exciting. On the other hand, they also made it so that the only alternative to being in the Hitler Youth was to be against it. This opened the way for youth gangs, which eventually became more common in the Third Reich than they had been in the Weimar Republic. A strange record for a régime which aimed at capturing the support of the whole of Germany's youth!

QUESTIONS

1. How did the Nazis try to influence German youth?
2. Why do you think the picture Source L was taken?
3. If the Hitler Youth was so popular, why did many young people oppose it?

4.3 How did life change for women and the family?

The treatment of women in the Third Reich

The Nazis had definite ideas about the role of women in society: their place was very much in the home, as child-bearers and supporters of their husbands (Source A). Women had a role which was entirely separate from that of men and there was therefore no question of equality: they were different. As a result of these views, women were squeezed out of a large number of jobs shortly after Hitler came to power. The first to go were women doctors and civil servants. The number of women teachers declined, and no more were admitted to lectureships at universities. From 1936 no woman could be a judge or prosecutor and they were even removed from jury service, on the grounds that they would be unable to think logically and without emotion.

Source A

▲ A Nazi propaganda poster showing how the Nazis saw the role of women.

How did women react?

Since women represent a broad cross-section of society, they reacted in different ways. Some had always believed their role was a domestic one and would have voted for Hitler in the first place. Others might well have been converted to the Nazi idea and were proud of the new status given to motherhood. Many perhaps were resentful, but accepted their role because they had no choice. But there were some who protested. A few women joined opposition groups like the Communists or Social Democrats. A large number, however, actually worked from within the system. Although in every other respect they were loyal Nazis, they criticized the policy towards women on three grounds. First, many women would remain unfulfilled. Second, women were being deprived of experience which was vital for them. Third, women had particular talents for certain types of employment.

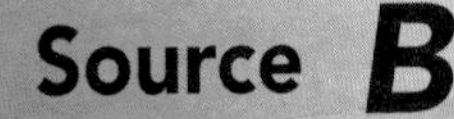

Source B

Woman has the task of being beautiful and bringing children into the world . . . The female bird preens herself for her mate and hatches her eggs for him.

▲ Goebbels' view of the role of women.

Source C

Equal rights for women means that they receive the esteem they deserve in the sphere nature has assigned to them.

▲ Hitler's views on 'equality' for women.

Did the Nazis modify their policy? Those women who protested were usually disciplined and there were few changes in the regulations which prevented women from joining the professions. On the other hand, more and more women were employed as factory workers by the end of the 1930s and certainly during the Second World War. This was largely because there was a shortage of labour and women had the special advantage to employers of being cheaper. They were paid less than men and usually carried out the menial tasks.

Did the family benefit from Nazi rule?

The family was given a special place in the Nazi state and was frequently publicized in photographs like Source G. The family fulfilled two main purposes. First, it was the basic social unit in which Nazi ideas would be put into practice. Second, it was the means by which Hitler would achieve one of his main objectives – the rapid expansion of the German population.

The Nazis banned birth control clinics, contraception and abortion. They encouraged large families through financial inducements like marriage loans, family allowances and child subsidies. The Nazis also used propaganda to increase the birth rate. The word 'family' was only given to households with four or more children, and women were encouraged to be 'blessed with children' (*kindersegen*). An award was provided for mothers who had had many children: the **Honour Cross of the German Mother**, with a gold cross for those with more than eight. At the other extreme, they encouraged childless couples to divorce so that the fertile partner could have a chance of children in the future.

Whether these measures benefited the family is a matter of opinion, and certain questions need to be asked. Is it always good to have a large family? What are the implications of preventing birth control? Do families always have to include children? There were also other controls on families which some people would have found distressing.

Source D

We see our daughters growing up in stupid aimlessness, living only in the vain hope of perhaps getting a man and having children. If they do not succeed, their lives will be thwarted.

▲ **View of some German women, 1934.**

Source E

It is a regrettable fact that a war of the sexes is raging inside the teaching profession. Not only have women teachers a right to their own existence, but bringing up children requires the best possible training of mothers.

▲ **Head of the women's section of the Nazi Teachers' Organization.**

Source F

Women doctors could give aid and comfort to fatigued mothers. Women teachers would be most suited to instruct adolescent girls Women jurists would be most qualified for dealing with cases involving children.

▲ **The view of a Nazi feminist, Sophie Rogge-Berne in 1937.**

Effects on family life

To preserve the purity of the racial stock, anyone suffering a hereditary defect such as mental illness, epilepsy or blindness, was sterilized. The pressures put upon couples to have children might also have been psychologically damaging. We might also consider the effects on family life of other policies of the Nazis. Children were so active that they had very little home life. How often would the fathers, with their increased workload, have been at home to enjoy family life? And how would mothers have dealt with young boys who were taught to believe that women should always be subservient?

Source G

▲ **A Nazi official and his family.**

Source H

I think one of the worst effects of the whole Nazi Youth movement is that our children no longer get any peace or quiet, and I dread to think the kind of people they will grow up into if they are subject to this incessant thundering of propaganda all the time.

▲ **How a German mother felt about the Hitler Youth. From E. Amy Buller, *Darkness over Germany*, 1945.**

QUESTIONS

1. What do Sources A, B and C on page 71 tell us about Nazi policies towards women?
2. 'It was not possible to be a good Nazi and a believer in the rights of women'. Do the sources in this section support this view?
3. Look at Source G. Using the other information and sources on pages 71–2, do you think it gives a reliable picture of the family in Nazi Germany?
4. Did Nazi policies benefit the family? Explain your answer.

4.4 What was it like to be a minority group in Nazi Germany?

Recently there has been an increased interest in those people living in the Third Reich who were seen as 'social outcasts'. These were minority groups. Source A shows that historians now aim to look at the conditions experienced by all such peoples.

Who were the minorities?

The Nazis considered that 'social outcasts' were all groups who in any way threatened the 'purity' of the Aryan race. There were several of these, all completely separate from each other. They were, however, linked together by the persecution they experienced.

- **Jews**. The Jewish people had always been the main target of Nazi persecution. There must, however, have been some confusion among Jews about Hitler's real intentions towards them, and hopes that he did not mean what he had written in *Mein Kampf*. They experienced relatively peaceful periods followed by sudden upturns in persecution. Between 1933 and 1934 Hindenburg stopped some of the more extreme measures. But then came the **Nuremberg Laws** of 1935. Things seemed to improve in 1936, when many of the public signs against Jews were removed. But this was only because of the **Olympic Games**, held in Berlin that year.

  Persecution began again in 1937 and was intensified with *Kristallnacht* in 1938. By 1941 Jewish people assumed that there were further measures in store for them – but most believed that this would mean resettlement somewhere outside Germany. What actually happened was the Holocaust (see pages 84–6).

- **Gypsies**. Their mixed race and travelling lifestyle made gypsies a double target; the Nazis considered them racially impure and idle. Gypsies faced two large attacks on their personal freedom. They were made to give up travelling which was their whole way of life. And they were prevented from having families by being sterilized. Most gypsies were eventually exterminated alongside Jews.

- **The insane**. Those who were mentally ill, were also considered a threat to Aryan purity. The first step was to sterilize such patients, while later measures included euthanasia or 'mercy killing', by means of injection or carbon monoxide gas.

- **Tramps and beggars**. What separated tramps and beggars from the rest of society is that they had no fixed home or work. This might be through circumstance or choice. In a democracy efforts are made to provide housing and employment but ultimately the choice is there: a tramp may remain a tramp.

Source A

Of all Nazi atrocities, the extermination of the Jews has, rightly, commanded the most attention from historians and the general public. But this understandable preoccupation with the horrors of Nazi anti-Semitism has led people to overlook the fact that the Jews formed only one, albeit the major, target in a broad campaign directed against a variety of groups who were considered to be 'alien to the community'.

▲ **An article by Jeremy Noakes in *History Today*, 1985.**

Source B

The gypsy question can only be regarded as solved when the majority . . . have been brought together in large camps and made to work and when the continual procreation of this half-breed population has been finally prevented. Only then will future generations be freed from this burden.

▲ **A chilling comment by Robert Ritter, a Nazi, on how gypsies should be treated.**

In Nazi Germany this choice was removed. Such people were called 'community aliens'. They were forcibly integrated, or removed. Most tramps and beggars had already been rounded up from 1933. Up to 500,000 tramps and beggars were put to forced labour. Many were sterilized, the assumption being that they would 'pollute' German women.

- **Homosexuals**. Homosexuality was despised by the Nazis, since it went against their vision of Aryan manhood. This was despite the fact that there were many homosexuals in the SA, including Röhm himself. They, of course, were protected by being members of a huge organization which chose to ignore their activities. Individual homosexuals led a life of fear. They were often informed upon. They would then be arrested by the Gestapo and sent to one of the concentration camps, where they were made to wear a pink identification badge. They were often beaten up by other prisoners and many were compulsorily sterilized. This was as much a punishment as a precaution.

- **Alcoholics**. In a democracy, alcoholism is not an offence, although it might lead to an action which is. In Nazi Germany much was done to discourage heavy drinking and there was a decline in alcohol consumption. This made it easier to identify alcoholics. Suspects were humiliated by having their heads shaved. Persistent offenders were sent to concentration camps.

Source C

In the case of community aliens who are only a burden on the national community welfare is not necessary, rather police compulsion with the aim of either making them once more useful members of the national community through appropriate measures or of preventing them from being a further burden.

▲ **A police order to deal with 'community aliens', 1940.**

QUESTIONS

1 What kinds of people did the Nazis refer to as 'community aliens'?

2 Which other minority groups suffered under the Nazis?

3 Why would many Jewish people find themselves confused about the real intentions of the Nazis?

4 Why did the Nazis object to gypsies, tramps, beggars, homosexuals and alcoholics?

4.5 What did the German people think of Hitler?

Throughout his period in power, Hitler was considerably more popular than the Nazi Party. Lloyd George (Source A) commented that Hitler was trusted by the old and idolized by the young.

There has been much discussion about this, but one of the best explanations has been provided by Ian Kershaw, a British historian. Kershaw identifies two reasons for the widespread acceptance of Hitler: his image and the need the people felt they had for him (see Source B on page 76).

Source A

It is true that that public criticism of the [German] Government is forbidden in every form. That does not mean the criticism is absent. I have heard the speeches of Nazi orators freely condemned.

But not a word of criticism or of disapproval have I heard of Hitler.

▲ **An article by David Lloyd George, former British Prime Minister, in the *Daily Express*, 1936.**

The image of Hitler

There had always been a strong tradition of right-wing leadership in Germany. During the 18th century Prussia had risen to be a major military power under Frederick the Great (1740–88). Germany was united in 1871 by **Bismarck**, who became Chancellor until 1890. The new state was ruled by a Kaiser (Emperor), the last of whom was Wilhelm II. Frederick the Great, Bismarck and Wilhelm II were all considered to be heroic figures in German history, and in some ways Hitler was their natural successor. But Hitler had an additional advantage: whereas the others had represented only a small part of society, Hitler was seen as a 'man of the people'.

During the 1930s Hitler did everything possible to put across this image. His portrait was commissioned from one of the leading Nazi artists, **Heinrich Knirr** (Source D).

Hitler developed highly effective speaking techniques. He purposely arrived late to build up the tension of the crowd and used a few highly effective gestures. He started quietly, built up to a climax and then repeated the process. His voice was known throughout Germany because there was a radio in every home. In addition to this, the population would have been indoctrinated into accepting his ideas, by the techniques described on pages 43–5. Many people therefore reacted to him with enthusiasm and adulation.

Source B

For almost a decade after 1933, Hitler enjoyed a remarkable degree of popularity among the great majority of the German people . . . What seems necessary is an examination not of Hitler's personality, but of his popular image – how the German people saw their leader: the 'Hitler myth'. The Hitler myth was double-sided. On the one hand it was a masterly achievement in image-building by the new techniques of propaganda . . . On the other hand, it has to be seen as a reflection of 'mentalities' and values . . . which conditioned the acceptance of a 'Superman' image of political leadership.

▲ **An extract from a recent article by the British historian, Ian Kershaw, in *History Today*.**

Source C

► **Hitler speaking in 1933.**

Source D

▲ A portrait of Hitler, painted by Heinrich Knirr, 1937.

Source E

▲ Hitler idolized by crowds.

▼ Hitler idolized by youth.

Source F

The appeal to a German need

The overall situation in which Germany found itself after 1929 worked in Hitler's favour. This continued to be the case. Although some Germans opposed Hitler, most saw him as the direct answer to their needs. He would restore political order after the chaos of the Weimar Republic. He would reduce unemployment. The middle classes relied upon him to end profiteering capitalism; the industrialists expected him to destroy communism. He would also restore Germany's prestige abroad and end the shame of Versailles. In short, he would restore purpose to a nation which had lost its direction.

4.6 Exercise: Book-burning and the control of knowledge

1 Look at Source 1. Why did the Nazis encourage young people to burn books? Think about Nazi policies towards young people in your answer.

2 What does Source 2 tell you about life in Germany under the Nazis?

3 The Nazis could easily have removed Jewish books from libraries without making such a fuss. Why, then, did they organize public book-burnings?

Source 1

▲ Hitler Youth helping to burn books and pictures in Salzburg in 1938.

Source 2

The 'shame' of which my father spoke was the Nazis' book-burning, which Dr Barsch had chosen to describe as a glorius occasion. On the evening of 10 May, book-burnings had taken place in front of the Humboldt University in Berlin and in many other university towns. The works of all Jewish authors were tossed into flames, as were the writings of others who for one reason or another were hated by the Nazis. The list of nearly twenty thousand writers included almost every important name in German letters [literature].

▲ A description by Bernt Engelmann, a German anti-Nazi resistance worker. Dr Barsch was a former family friend who worked for a newspaper. He claimed he was forced to write an article praising the book-burnings. From *In Hitler's Germany*, published in 1986.

Source 3

The soul of the German people can again express itself. These flames do not only cast light on the end of an old era. They also light up the new one.

▲ Dr Joseph Goebbels, speaking at a bonfire of books in Berlin on 10 May 1933. Over 20,000 books were burned, including many by Germany's most famous authors.

Source 4

A huge bonfire of books judged by the Nazis to be 'un-German' is burning tonight in the square in front of Berlin University. A similar bonfire burnt in Munich where thousands of school children watched. . . 'As you watch the fire burn these un-German books', the children were told, 'let it also burn into your hearts love of the Fatherland' . . . New books ordered by the libraries are to be by writers unknown abroad and, from their titles, seem to be novels written to glorify war.

▲ A report by an English newspaper about the book burning in Germany in May 1933.

CHAPTER 5

THE IMPACT OF WAR ON THE THIRD REICH

5.1 Hitler's attitude to war

A century and a half before Hitler invaded Poland in 1939, a Prussian military strategist, **Karl von Clausewitz**, wrote a book on the meaning of war. It shocked many at the time by its frankness. Clausewitz said that war was a means of getting what politicians could not achieve by peaceful methods. In one respect, however, Clausewitz was fairly traditional. For him, as for most other people, war was an exceptional period, an emergency which a country had to go through from time to time.

Hitler changed this attitude. He believed that the most basic influence in life was struggle. The highest form of struggle in its human form was war, which was therefore a natural condition. It was inevitable that a vigorous race would want to increase the territory it controlled, at the expense of weaker races. In the case of Germany, the most obvious area for future expansion was eastwards at the expense of **Poland** and the **Soviet Union**.

With the four statements shown in Sources B–E, Hitler turned the whole attitude to war inside out. Instead of being an exception, it became the norm. Nazi Germany therefore became a state which geared itself to war.

Source A

War is the continuation of policy [diplomacy] by other means.

▲ From *On War* by Karl von Clausewitz (1780–1831). The ideas in this book, published in 1833, dominated military thinking until the First World War.

Source B

It has always been the right of the stronger, before God and man, to see his will prevail. All of nature is one great struggle between strength and weakness, an eternal victory of the strong over the weak.

▲ Hitler's views on struggle, from a speech made in 1923.

Source C

War is the most natural, the most ordinary thing. War is constant; war is everywhere. There is no beginning, there is no conclusion of peace. War is life. All struggle is war.

▲ Adolf Hitler, *Mein Kampf*, 1925.

Source D

We put a stop to the eternal movement of the Germanic people to Europe's South and West and we turn our eyes to the land in the East.

▲ Adolf Hitler, *Mein Kampf*, 1925.

Source E

According to an eternal law of Nature, the right to the land belongs to the one who conquers the land because the old boundaries did not yield sufficient space for the growth of the population. Every healthy, vigorous people sees nothing sinful in territorial expansion, but something quite in keeping with its nature.

▲ Extracts from Hitler's *Second Book*, 1928.

5.2 How did the people adjust to the experience of war?

The Second World War falls into two main stages for Germany. Up to 1941 German armies were triumphant and most German civilians suffered few ill-effects from being at war. From 1941, however, the struggle intensified, the number of military defeats increased and civilians experienced hardship.

Blitzkrieg 1939–41

For many Germans, the early experience of war was exhilarating. In September 1939 they read about the conquest of Poland in the newspapers and saw newsreels showing German tanks and aircraft meeting virtually no resistance. However, most people were worried about what would happen when Germany finally engaged Britain and France in the West. After all, during the First World War (1914–18), French and British armies had stopped the German advance.

In fact, when the time came, Hitler conquered much of western Europe with surprising ease. In 1940 he took Denmark, Norway, Holland, Belgium and Luxembourg. But the real prize was France, which was conquered by German panzer divisions within a matter of weeks in June 1940. The German people were delirious that such opposition had been destroyed so easily and they were swept along with the success of *Blitzkrieg*. They were bombarded with films showing the collapse of the French armies and the triumphant march of the German army into Paris. Hitler had never before been so popular.

So far, all this had cost German civilians very little. The strategy of *Blitzkrieg* meant that they were not deprived of essentials. Instead, there was the prospect that Germany would grow ever richer and that each new conquest would expand the economic base further. Hitler himself helped spread such ideas with vivid accounts of future German settlements in eastern Europe. The overall feeling most Germans had was how easy it had all been.

Total war 1941–5

This did not, of course last. In 1941 Hitler greatly extended Germany's commitments. He put off his plans to invade Britain and decided to turn eastwards and invade the Soviet Union instead.

Source A

▲ **The weapons of *Blitzkrieg*.**

Source B

It is safe to say that the entire nation is filled with a believing trust in the Führer such as has never before existed to this extent.

▲ **Said by the district leader of Augsburg, 1940.**

Source C

The 'Reich Farmers' are to live in extraordinarily beautiful settlements [in eastern Europe]. The German officers and authorities are to have splendid buildings, the governors are to have palaces.

▶ **From Hitler's *Table Talk*, 1942.**

At first the German armies were brilliantly successful and succeeded in taking a large part of the Soviet Union. Then the **Red Army** fought back and eventually overwhelmed Germany. By 1942 the Soviet Union was already out-producing Germany in all types of armaments. The German armies were being held and driven back.

The civilian population in Germany suddenly found that war involved longer working hours, severe food rationing and very heavy losses among troops on the Eastern Front. Almost every family experienced bereavement after the end of 1942. The German government conducted a propaganda campaign to raise morale. One element of this was a series of posters claiming that victory for Germany was certain in the long run.

In 1943 Goebbels made a brilliant speech at the Berlin Sports Palace (Sources F and G). In it he sold the German people the idea of **total war**, as opposed to the easy victories which *Blitzkrieg* had produced.

Source D

	Germany	USSR
Tanks	9,300	24,700
Aircraft	14,700	25,400
Artillery	12,000	127,000

▲ **German and Soviet arms production, 1942.**

Source E

▲ **A Nazi propaganda poster of 1942: 'Victory will be ours!'**

Source F

I ask you: Do you believe with the Führer and with us in the final total victory of the German people? I ask you: Are you determined to follow the Führer through thick and thin in the struggle for victory and to put up even with the heaviest personal burdens?

I ask you: Do you want total war? Do you want it, if necessary, more total and more radical than we can even imagine it today?

▲ **Goebbels' speech on total war in the Berlin Sports Palace, 1943.**

Source G

▲ **A photograph of the audience listening to Goebbels' speech in the Berlin Sports Palace, 1943.**

His speech received the overwhelming support of the audience, and newsreels of the occasion were shown throughout Germany.

Throughout 1943 and 1944 the German people had to endure constant and very heavy bombing by British and American aircraft. One city after another was destroyed: Munich, Nuremberg, Cologne, Essen, Dortmund and above all, Hamburg, Dresden and Berlin.

The attacks were intended to weaken civilian morale, although there is no evidence that it was any more successful than Hitler's efforts to break Londoners in the **Blitz** of 1941. If anything, civilian bravery in Germany – as in Britain – demonstrated that they had finally made the adjustment to total war and being exposed to danger as direct as that experienced by any army.

But total war did not bring the success that the propaganda campaign had promised and internal resistance increased steadily.

Source H

Many German cities presented partial areas of vast devastation. Perhaps the outstanding example was Hamburg, where a series of attacks in July and August of 1943 destroyed 55 to 60 per cent of the city, did damage to an area of 30 square miles; completely burned out 12.5 square miles, wiped out 300,000 dwelling units and made 75,000 people homeless. German estimates range from 60,000 to 100,000 persons killed, many of them in shelters where they were reached by carbon-monoxide poisoning. The attacks used both high-explosive and incendiary bombs as it was thought by the Air Forces and later confirmed that the former created road blocks, broke water mains, disrupted communications, opened buildings, broke windows, and displaced roofing. Most important, they kept the fire fighters in shelters until the incendiaries became effective. But, of the total destruction, 75 to 80 per cent was due to fires, particularly to those in which the so-called fire storm phenomenon was observed.

▲ **Report from the US strategic bombing survey, 30 September 1945.**

Source I

▲ **The destruction of Dresden by Allied bombing, February 1945.**

QUESTIONS

1. Describe and explain the success of the German forces between 1939 and 1941.
2. Why was 1941 a turning point in the Second World War?
3. Study Sources H and I. Why did such a level of destruction not lead to Germany's surrender? Use the text on pages 81–2 and Sources E, F and G in your answer.

5.3 War and the Holocaust

Before the outbreak of war, the Nazis had confined their measures against the Jews to discrimination and occasional instances of organized violence such as *Kristallnacht* (page 55). From 1939, however, war brought further changes and made anti-Semitic policies even more extreme.

From 1941 onwards, for example, the Nazis came up with the '**Final Solution**'. In addition to the original concentration camps, a number of new extermination camps were set up, mainly in occupied Poland. Here over six million Jews were murdered between 1941 and 1945. The details were settled on 20 January 1942 at the **Wannsee Conference** in Berlin, which envisaged the killing of all Jews in German-occupied Europe.

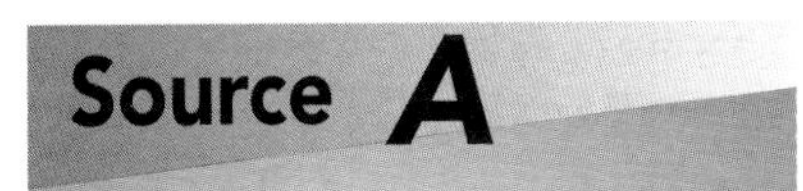

Fundamental to National Socialist genocide was Hitler's race dogma.

▲ **Klaus Hildebrand, a German historian, in 1984.**

How did the war affect the treatment of the Jews?

The 'Final Solution' might appear to be one issue on which historians are unanimous. Yet there are disagreements, especially among German historians. One debate is on whether the killing of the Jews was always Hitler's *intention* or whether it was *actually caused by the war*. Klaus Hildebrand, and others, argue that Hitler's ideas, written in *Mein Kampf*, were directly responsible for the **genocide**, or mass-killing of the Jews, and that this was always his eventual aim (Source A).

The extermination of the Jews came about, it would seem, not only because of the professed intention to destroy them but also as a way out of the impasse [dead end] into which the régime had manoeuvred itself.

▲ **Martin Broszat, a German historian, in 1981.**

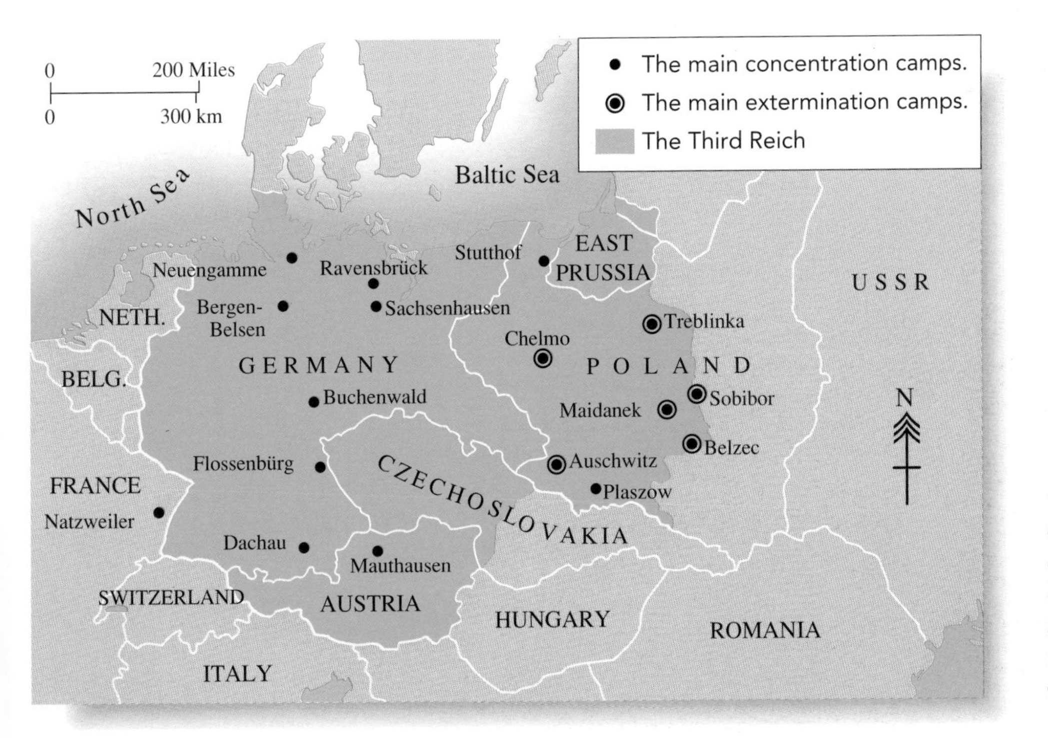

◀ **Nazi concentration and extermination camps in Germany and German-occupied territories.**

Source C

I was ordered to establish extermination facilities at Auschwitz in June 1942. When I set up the extermination building at Auschwitz, I used Cyclon B, which was a crystallised prussic acid which we dropped into the death chamber from a small opening. It took from three to fifteen minutes to kill the people in the death chamber, depending on the climatic conditions. We knew when the people were dead because their screaming stopped. We usually waited about half an hour before we opened the doors and removed the bodies . . . Our special squads took off the rings and extracted the gold from the teeth of the corpses.

▲ **A description, by Rudolf Hoess, of the methods of killing Jews at Auschwitz.**

On the other hand, Martin Broszat (Source B on page 83) argues that more important than Hitler's intentions was the influence of the war. The Nazis had put themselves in a position which led directly to genocide. At the end of this section you will be asked to weigh up these views.

But whether or not Hitler always intended to exterminate the Jewish people, we can certainly see the war acting as a catalyst: that is to say, it speeded up the measures against the Jews and led directly to the Holocaust.

- In the first place, it closed off one of the options which Hitler had been considering – moving the whole Jewish population to another area, such as the island of Madagascar. This would not be possible in wartime.
- Second, the German conquest of eastern Europe opened up huge new concentrations of Jews in Poland and the Soviet Union.
- Third, German armed forces and the SS came into direct contact with these people and had to make a decision on how to treat them. Instructions were issued to the SS to kill as many as possible, although many of the army officers were unhappy about this policy.
- Fourth, it was possible in wartime to pursue policies which would have been more difficult in peace. The wartime emergency made it possible to keep the extermination secret from the majority of the population.

Source D

► **The remains of ovens at Auschwitz, which were used to cremate the bodies of people killed in the gas chambers. This photograph was taken in 1995.**

The Holocaust

The Nazis used two main forms of mass-murder in the territories they occupied, especially in eastern Europe.

The first was special SS detachments with machine guns. These operated throughout the western Soviet Union, especially in the Ukraine.

The second was the use of gas chambers in the extermination camps set up in Poland at Treblinka, Maidanek, Chelmo, Sobibor and, above all, Auschwitz, in which camp alone over two million people were killed by the SS. The commandant of Auschwitz, **Rudolf Hoess**, later provided evidence at Nuremberg about how the gassings were carried out. He described how: '*We tried to fool the victims into thinking they were going through a delousing process. At times they realized our intentions and we had riots and difficulties.*' The bodies were then disposed of in ovens which were specially made by leading German manufacturers. Auschwitz was also the scene of cruel and pointless medical experiments carried out by **Josef Mengele**, an SS doctor (Source E).

Source E

I have never accepted that Mengele himself believed he was doing serious medical work . . . He was only exercising his power.

Mengele ran a butcher shop – major surgeries were performed without anaesthesia. Once I witnessed a stomach operation. Mengele was removing pieces from the stomach, but without any anaesthesia. Another time, it was the heart that was removed, again, without anaesthesia. It was horrifying.

▲ **The memories of Alex Dekel, a Romanian Jew who was himself experimented on at Auschwitz.**

Lest we forget . . .

Several organizations exist today to remind the world of what the Jews and others experienced in the Holocaust. Why should this be the case?

There have always been those who have either tried to cover up the extermination programme, or who have denied that it ever existed. **Heinrich Himmler**, the SS leader, considered that it should always be kept secret.

Terms like 'resettled', 'evacuated' or 'deported' could be used to describe what had happened to the Jews. **Heydrich**, Himmler's deputy, had already given orders in 1941 that the killing of Jews should only be photographed or filmed by officials and that the results would be a state secret. After the war many former Nazis denied that the Holocaust had ever happened.

A similar line has been taken more recently by a British historian, David Irving. He has claimed that Hitler gave no orders for the extermination of Jews. It is true, he says, that many Jews were shot, but this was no more horrific than the Allied bombing of Dresden. To the vast majority of historians, however, the Holocaust remains the worst case of genocide ever committed – and there have been many.

Let me, in all frankness, mention a terribly hard chapter to you. Among ourselves we can talk openly about it, though we will never speak a word of it in public . . . I am speaking about the evacuation of the Jews, the extermination of the Jewish people . . . That is a page of glory in our history that never has been and never will be written.

▲ **Himmler speaking to a meeting of SS officers in 1943.**

Anne Frank and Rudolf Hoess

Two people received a great deal of publicity after the end of the War. One was Anne Frank, an innocent victim of the persecution organized by the Nazis. The other was Rudolf Hoess, one of the organizers, who claimed to be a 'normal' human being and himself a victim of the system.

ANNE FRANK (1929–45)

Anne Frank was a Jewish schoolgirl who was born in Frankfurt. Her family fled to Holland from Nazi persecution. When the Nazis occupied Holland and started to round up the Jews there, her family and friends went into hiding in a sealed-off set of rooms at the top of an office block in Amsterdam, where they remained for two years. The family was eventually betrayed to the security police, who raided the hiding place in August 1944. The Franks were sent to various concentration camps, Anne to Auschwitz and then to Bergen-Belsen where, in March 1945, she died – only weeks before the end of the War. She is remembered through her diary, which she kept throughout her period in hiding. This was found by her father in 1945 and eventually published. Source G, which is an extract from this diary, expresses the hurt which Jewish people felt at being singled out for such persecution.

RUDOLF HOESS (1900–47)

A leading member of the SS, Hoess became the commandant at Auschwitz extermination camp in 1940. He was directly responsible for the gassing and shooting of over two million people. He went into hiding at the end of the War but was captured by Allied military police in 1946.

He was put on trial in Poland for crimes against humanity and executed in March 1947. During his trial much new evidence came out about conditions at Auschwitz and about the medical experiments of Mengele. Hoess always claimed that he was a normal, happily married family man, and that he was acting on orders.

Source G

Our many Jewish friends are being taken away by the dozen. These people are being treated by the Gestapo without a shred of decency. . . It is impossible to escape; most of the people in the camp are branded as inmates by their shaven heads. . . If it is as bad as this in Holland whatever will it be like in the distant and barbarous regions they are sent to?

▲ **Extract from the *Diary of Anne Frank*, 9 October 1942, describing life for Jews outside their 'secret annex'.**

Source H

I am completely normal. Even while I was carrying out the task of extermination I led a normal family life. I never grew indifferent to human suffering. I have always seen and felt for it . . . From our entire training the thought of refusing an order just didn't enter one's head, regardless of what kind of order it was.

▲ **Rudolf Hoess's description of himself.**

QUESTIONS

1. Using the text and sources on pages 83–6 explain why some historians think 'The Final Solution' was always Hitler's aim, but others think he only put it into operation because of the War.
2. 'Anne Frank and Rudolf Hoess were both victims of the Nazi system'. Do you agree with this?

5.4 Life in the Ghetto of Lodz

This section is a study of the life of a Jewish community during the period of the Holocaust.

In September 1939, the Germans occupied and incorporated half of Poland into the Reich. They immediately began to apply the anti-Semitic laws with maximum rigour. Poland had over three million Jews, far more than any other country in Europe. Many lived in Jewish quarters in the major cities such as Warsaw and Lodz. These were now converted by the Nazis into sealed **ghettoes**. Jews were prevented from leaving these ghettoes by armed guards, walls and barbed wire. Wherever Jews had to cross a street inhabited by non-Jews, special bridges were constructed. The plan opposite shows how the ghetto in Lodz related to the rest of the city.

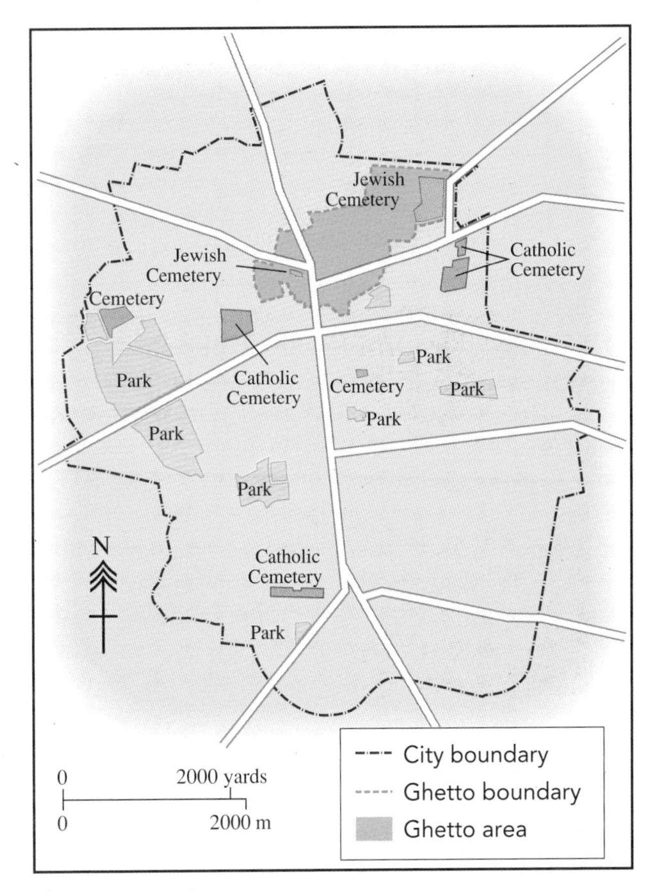

▲ **The city of Lodz in 1939 showing the location of the ghetto area.**

The Ghetto of Lodz

The Germans used Lodz in several ways. First, it became a centre for many Jews brought in from Germany and Austria. The population therefore increased for a while and overcrowding was a serious problem. Later, people were moved out to unknown destinations; Lodz was therefore a staging post to the death camps of **Auschwitz** and **Chelmno** which were not far away. By the end of 1944 the ghetto was deserted. Finally, the Germans used Jewish labour. Some of the people of Lodz worked in the many small factories and workshops inside the ghetto, producing a variety of materials and clothes. Others provided the Nazis with manual labour working on projects outside the ghetto.

The brutal Nazi governor of Poland, **Hans Frank**, set up his early headquarters in Lodz. The German occupiers issued a series of instructions and regulations to be observed by the Jewish people. The ghetto itself was, however, administered by senior members of the Jewish community. They did what they could to reduce the harshness of the conditions in the ghetto. Their rule was certainly far better than a direct German occupation of the ghetto, even though they had to act on German instructions.

Source A

Children born in 1935 are to be integrated into the workshop labour force.
The endurance of men hiding from conscription for outside labour is as great as their fear of being despatched from the ghetto. They draw no rations because their food cards have been invalidated; and the same holds true for their families.

▲ **Extracts from the *Chronicle of the Ghetto of Lodz* for Monday 21 February, 1944**

The *Chronicle of the Ghetto of Lodz*

A *Chronicle*, written by several people between January 1941 and 1944, provides us with valuable information about conditions in the ghetto. Its existence was probably known to the Jewish administration, but almost certainly not to the Germans. Even so, the writers were careful not to criticize any of the authorities – Jewish or German. Most of the articles were about everyday life in the ghetto. The most important articles, however, concerned work and **deportation**.

The children of the Ghetto of Lodz

Children in the ghetto were put to work in small factories by order of the Germans. Most of them worked as tailors and seamstresses. Their education suffered and they experienced all the stresses of adults. Special classes, however, were set up to try to provide education and possibly to relieve the stress the children must have experienced. These would have been conducted secretly, within the factories.

These classes may have used drawings and verses of the type shown in Sources C and D. The authors were anonymous, but the pictures and words are in the style of a children's book. They relate to life in the Lodz ghetto but also have images of the fairy tale with which young children would normally have been familiar.

Source B

There were about 40 children in every course. Working in the classroom was very hard for the pupils and for the teachers. The room was fairly small, and there was constant tension, fear of a surprise German inspection, and concern that informers would tell the Germans about this educational activity. Whenever a German team came into the factory, the children would instantly turn the room into a work area.

▲ **From Sara Grober, *Jewish Public Activities in the Lodz Ghetto*, 1979.**

QUESTIONS

1 Suggest reasons for people wanting to produce **a** the *Lodz Chronicle* and **b** the pictures and verse in Sources C and D.

2 How useful are such sources to the historian studying the plight of Jews after 1939?

3 Why would the children's classes have been held within the ghetto factories?

Source C

The naughty dwarfs
Such wise guys
Always wrecking her stitches...
Hey, the difficulties disappeared!
The pranksters no longer interfere.
The children are pleasured . . .
Flee sadness! Go away!
Joy is ours!

Source D

Dawn ... behind the hill the sun thrusts its rays.
Behind the bushes here and there shadows play,
And slowly disappear.
The sun with golden glow lights up the mountain peak
and then just a minute later
Heads of flowers peek from twixt the blades of grass
And see a castle, as in legends.

▲ **Pictures and verse produced in the Lodz Ghetto.**

5.5 Resistance to Hitler during the War

We have seen that there was opposition to Nazi rule during the 1930s. This was dealt with by the growth of the **totalitarian state**. During the first two years of the War, there was very little opposition but, from 1941, it re-emerged and aimed at overthrowing the Nazi régime altogether. For this reason it is more appropriate to call it *resistance*. This resistance took a variety of forms.

Student resistance

White Rose was a group of students at the University of Munich. They were led by Hans and Sophie Scholl and Professor Kurt Huber. They spread leaflets and posters appealing for passive resistance to the Nazi régime: people could help by refusing to co-operate with the Party.

Conservative resistance

Another group consisted of people who had once been prepared to tolerate the Nazis but who had become disillusioned with Hitler's policies and above all the War. **Ulrich von Hassell** had been Hitler's ambassador in Rome, while **Carl Goerdeler** had been a strong opponent of the Weimar Republic. Goerdeler hoped that if Hitler was replaced, the Allies would let Germany return to the frontiers it had held before the Treaty of Versailles. The Allies, however, consistently demanded **unconditional surrender**.

Christian resistance

Many Christians – both Protestant and Catholic – tried to resist Nazi policies. Especially important was the **Kreisau Circle**, which produced a programme called the *Principles for the New Order of Germany*, which they hoped would replace the Nazi régime.

Military resistance

The army was in the best position to try to remove Hitler's régime. Some, like General Beck, had already tried to do this in 1938. They were joined after 1941 by others, such as Field Marshal Rommel and Admiral Canaris. The most famous attempt was the bomb placed by **Count von Stauffenberg** in Hitler's military headquarters in East Prussia on 20 July 1944. Although the bomb exploded, Hitler escaped with minor wounds. Four of Hitler's military advisers were killed. All those involved in the conspiracy were hanged with piano wire.

The day of reckoning has come, the day when German youth will settle accounts with the vilest tyranny ever endured by our nation. In the name of German youth, we demand from Adolf Hitler's state the restoration of personal freedom, a German's most precious possession, which it took from us by base deceit . . .

There can be but one word of action for us: Fight the party! Quit the party organizations, where all discussion is still being stifled. Each of us must join in the fight for our future.

▲ **Extracts from a White Rose pamphlet, 1943.**

Source B

The Government of the German Reich sees in Christianity the basis for the moral and religious revival of our people.

1. Justice which has been trampled under foot must be raised again and made predominant over all areas of human life.
2. Freedom of faith and of conscience will be safeguarded.
3. Totalitarian moral constraint must be broken and the inviolable dignity of the human person must be recognized as the basis for the order of justice and peace which is to be striven for.

▲ **The Kreisau Circle's *Principles for the New Order of Germany* issued on 9 August 1943.**

If the plot had been successful, the statement shown in Source C (opposite) would have been issued to the public.

Was there agreement?

What did the various parts of the resistance make of each other? Some favoured passive resistance, others preferred conspiracy and military-type violence to achieve their ends. Source D shows that von Hassell was deeply concerned about the different points of view and characters involved.

Perhaps the most respected of all the opponents was **Dietrich Bonhoeffer** (see below), who had contacts with most of the people mentioned.

DIETRICH BONHOEFFER (1906–45)

Bonhoeffer had studied theology at the Universities of Tübingen and Berlin, as well as in the USA. He was a German pastor of the Protestant Church, and from 1934 onwards opposed Hitler's policies towards the churches and minority groups. During the Second World War he collaborated with other opponents of the Nazis and tried to gain the co-operation of the Allies in a plot against Hitler. Many of the other conspirators saw Bonhoeffer as the best person to be German Chancellor after the assassination of Hitler. He was arrested by the Gestapo in April 1943 and sent to Flossenbürg concentration camp, where he was executed in 1945.

Source C

Germans:
Monstrous things have taken place under our eyes in the years past. Against the advice of all his experts, Hitler has unscrupulously sacrificed whole armies for his desire for glory . . . to maintain his power, he has established an unbridled reign of terror, destroying justice, banishing decency, . . . and destroying the happiness of millions.

We must not continue on that course! Having examined our conscience before God, we have assumed executive power . . . Without hatred, we will attempt the act of domestic conciliation. With dignity, we will attempt that of foreign conciliation.

▲ **Extracts from a statement which General Beck intended to make to the German people if Hitler had been assassinated, 1944.**

Source D

What has engrossed and disquieted me most during the past weeks has been the numerous conferences on questions concerning a change of régime. One major difficulty is Goerdeler. He . . . always sees things as he wishes to see them, and in many ways is a real reactionary.
The principal difficulty with Beck is that he is very theoretical . . . a man of tactics but little willpower, whereas Goerdeler has great willpower but no tactics.
I have always feared that we have too little contact with younger circles.

▲ **Entries in von Hassell's diary, December 1941. Von Hassell was arrested by the Nazis and executed on 8 September 1944.**

QUESTIONS

1. What different resistance groups developed in Germany after 1941?
2. Examine Sources A, B and C (pages 89–90). What do these groups have in common?
3. Did the resistance to Hitler fail only because it was too divided?

5.6 The end of the Third Reich

Defeat

Hitler had intended the Third Reich to last for a thousand years. In fact, it survived just twelve. The early triumphs of *Blitzkrieg* turned into the disasters of total war as the Germans were defeated at **Stalingrad** in the Soviet Union and **El Alamein** in North Africa (both in 1942). By the beginning of 1945 the British and Americans had occupied France and Italy, while the Red Army was driving German armies out of eastern Europe and had occupied Poland, Romania, Hungary and Czechoslovakia. Germany's cities had been wrecked by bombing and the Red Army was poised to take Berlin.

Source A

Wars are finally decided by one side or the other recognizing that they cannot be won. We must allow no moment to pass without showing the enemy that they can never reckon on our capitulation. Never!

▲ **Hitler, in his Will and Testament, April 1945.**

Source B

I have no successor. Hess is insane. Goering has lost the sympathy of the nation.

▲ **Hitler's Will and Testament, April 1945.**

Source C

It is untrue that I or anybody else in Germany wanted war in 1939. It was wanted and provoked entirely by those international statesmen who were either of Jewish origin or worked for Jewish interests.

▲ **Hitler's Will and Testament, April 1945.**

Hitler's attitude to defeat

Hitler refused to negotiate with the Allies or to make any realistic defence by pulling back his troops from the front. He blamed everyone else for the ruin which Germany now faced. He accused the German people of having gone soft and of being unworthy of victory. He considered that the other Nazi leaders were now useless. Finally, when the end was in sight, he returned to his more familiar theme of blaming the Jews for everything. At no time did he take any personal responsibility for Germany's destruction. Nor did he give a hint of regret for what had happened.

The end of the Third Reich

With the Red Army pounding Berlin, Hitler retreated to a fortified bunker under his Chancellery, where he decided to commit suicide. On 30 April 1945, therefore, Hitler took cyanide and, at the same time, shot himself. Goebbels ensured that the remains were burned, and then killed himself. The Third Reich survived Hitler for exactly one week and surrendered unconditionally on 7 May. Meanwhile, the British, American and Soviet troops had found the evidence of mass-killing and neglect in the extermination camps. The British, for example, liberated Bergen-Belsen, the Americans, Dachau and the Red Army, Auschwitz.

Justice?

The Allied armies were on the look out for all the Nazi leaders. Hitler, Goebbels and **Martin Bormann** had already committed suicide. Himmler took cyanide after being captured by the Americans. Many others, including Goering, Hess and Streicher were held in captivity. In November 1945 they were put on trial in Nuremberg and appeared before an international **tribunal** charged with war crimes and crimes against humanity. Over the following months many details emerged about the horrors of the death camps and Nazi persecution.

Source D

◀ The Nuremberg Tribunal in session in 1946.

Source E

It is my wish to be burned immediately in the place where I have carried out the greater part of my daily work during the course of my twelve years' service to my people.

▲ **From Hitler's last Will and Testament, April 1945.**

The most common defence heard in the court was that they were all 'obeying orders'. Some defendants, including Papen and Schacht, were acquitted. Others, like Hess and Speer, were sentence to terms of imprisonment. But most were sentenced to death and hanged. Goering managed to kill himself a few hours before his scheduled execution. The Tribunal ended in October 1946.

QUESTIONS

1. Why, in your opinion, did Hitler blame everyone but himself for the state Germany had reached by April 1945?
2. Was Hitler solely to blame for the state Germany was in by April 1945?
3. Describe what happened at the Nuremberg Tribunal using the text and Source D.

SUMMARY

- **1939–41** *Blitzkrieg.*
- **1939** Invasion of Poland.
- **1940** Conquest of Denmark, Norway, Netherlands, Belgium, France.
- **1940** Battle of Britain.
- **1941** Invasion of the USSR.
- **1941–5** Total war.
- **1942** Wannsee Conference on the extermination of the Jews (January). Turning points in the War: the Battles of Stalingrad and El Alamein.
- **1943–4** Heaviest Allied bombing of Germany.
- **1945** Allied discovery of the concentration and extermination camps.
- **1945** (April/May) Hitler's suicide and surrender of Germany.
- **1946** Nuremberg Tribunal.

5.7 Exercise: The German wartime 'Home Front'

Source 1

A certain air of modest prosperity pervaded the streets . . . Most were ready to admit that there was quite a lot to be said for the New Order . . . Look at young Heini, for instance, with his neatly clipped pate, so purposeful, so different from the long-haired lout who propped up the street corner some months back, and Father . . . with his [Nazi] Party badge.

▲ **Christabel Bielenberg, a young English woman married to a German lawyer, gives her impressions of how ordinary Germans viewed their country under the Nazi régime during the mid-1930s.**

Source 2

Though the outbreak of war was not greeted with popular enthusiasm, the extraordinary victories of 1939–42 were. The Führer seemed possessed of superhuman abilities. As victories changed to defeat, severe losses were experienced on the Russian front, German cities were pounded ceaselessly night and day by British and American planes and strict economic controls were enforced by Speer as he rapidly increased war production. Hitler disappeared from public view.

▲ **Modern historian Martin Roberts describing how defeats changed Germany during the course of the Second World War.**

Source 3

◀ **Bomb victims in Mannheim, 1944. By the end of the War many people lived in ruined buildings.**

1 Read Sources 1 and 4. Do you agree that these two sources show that in the mid-1930s the Nazis were loved by the German people, but by 1943 they were hated? Explain your answer.

2 a What do sources 2, 3 and 4 tell you about the effect of the War on German civilians?

b Using your own knowledge what other problems were caused for civilians by the War?

3 Why would Hitler have 'disappeared from public view' (Source 2) as soon as the bombing of German cities started and tighter restrictions came into force?

Source 4

Weds morning, 28 July 1943

There was no gas, no electricity, not a drop of water, neither the lift nor the telephone was working. It is hard to imagine the panic and chaos. There were no trams, no Underground, no rail-traffic to the suburbs. Most people loaded some belongings on carts, bicycles, prams, or carried things on their backs, and started on foot, just to get away, to escape. People who were wearing [Nazi] party badges had them torn off their coats and there were screams of 'Let's get that murderer'. The police did nothing.

▶ **A German eyewitness account of Hamburg on the morning after a heavy bombing raid.**

GLOSSARY

Anschluss the union of Austria and Germany. This was forbidden by the Treaty of Versailles but, in April 1938, German troops occupied Austria.

anti-Semitism a phrase used to describe hatred of Jewish people; first used in the late 19th century.

autobahn a 'superhighway' consisting of four lanes. Hitler carried out a programme of highway construction which, at its height, employed 70,000 people.

Bolsheviks a group, led by Lenin, which overthrew the Provisional Government in October 1917, and turned Russia into a communist country.

capitalism an economic system where industries and businesses are in the hands of private individuals. Powerful capitalists in Nazi Germany included Gustav Krupp and Fritz Thyssen who both owned large steelworks and supported Hitler.

degenerate art the name given by Hitler to forms of modern art which he disliked. Hitler confiscated over 12,000 paintings which he said were degenerate. Hitler approved of paintings which showed scenes such as Nazis marching.

demilitarize to keep free of soldiers and military installations. Under the Treaty of Versailles no German troops were allowed in the Rhineland (the part of Germany which directly bordered France).

encyclical the name given to a letter written by the Pope which is sent to Roman Catholic bishops.

Freikorps a group of former army officers and soldiers, established in 1919 after the First World War. They were anti-communist, anti-Jewish and nationalistic. Many Freikorps volunteers went on to join the SA.

Kreisau Circle a group of about twenty army officers and middle-class civilians set up in 1933 to oppose Hitler. They believed that the Nazis spelt disaster for Germany.

putsch an attempt to seize power using violence.

reparations payments made to the victorious nations of a war, to compensate for the damage done.

republic a country where there is no monarchy and the head of state is called a president.

Ruhr the most important coal mining and steel-making area in Germany. French troops invaded the Ruhr in January 1923 after the German government said it was unable to pay reparations.

Third Reich the word 'Reich' means 'empire'. The First Reich lasted from 962 until 1806. The Second Reich was set up by Otto von Bismarck in 1871. It lasted until 1918, when it was replaced by the Weimar Republic. The Third Reich was the Nazi régime of Hitler, which lasted from 1933–45.

totalitarian state a country where the government controls all aspects of life. There are no free elections. Secret police and censorship are used as instruments of control. Only one political party is permitted.

Wannsee Conference (1942) a meeting of fifteen senior Nazis, chaired by Reinhard Heydrich, and held in a suburb of Berlin called Grossen-Wannsee. The meeting decided to carry out the 'final solution of the Jewish question'.

Wall Street Crash the collapse of the American Stock Exchange, situated in Wall Street, New York, on 29 October 1929. The crash heralded the start of the Great Depression of the 1930s.

Wehrmacht the name given to the reorganized German armed forces set up in May 1935.

White Rose Movement a group of Munich students established in 1942, with the aim of opposing Hitler. The leaders were executed in 1943.

INDEX

Alsace-Lorraine 10
anti-Semitism 27, 29, 37, 52, 54–5
architecture 16–17, 58
art 16–17, 49, 56–7
Article 48 6, 19, 20, 38, 61
Auschwitz 84, 85–6, 87, 91
Austria, annexed by Germany (Anschluss) 55, 61
autarchy 61
autobahns 63, 66

Bamberg Conference (1926) 30, 38, 45
Bauhaus Movement 16–17
Bavaria 23–4, 30–1, 37
Beauty of Labour (SDA) 49, 65
Beck, Ludwig 51, 89, 90
Berlin 4, 23, 58
Bismarck, Otto von 76
Blitzkrieg 60–1, 80, 91, 92
Bonhoeffer, Dietrich 90
Bormann, Martin 91
Brüning, Heinrich 9, 19, 20, 22

capitalism 29, 33, 34, 76
Catholic Church and Nazism 50–1, 89
cinema 59
Clausewitz, Karl von 79
communism 29, 33, 34–5, 41, 76
concentration camps 46, 47, 59, 61, 75, 83, 85
Confessional Church 51

Dachau 47, 91
Dawes Plan (1924) 14, 22, 38
death's head units 46
democracy 6–7, 19, 38, 46–7
Depression (1930s) 18–19, 33, 35, 63
Drexler, Anton 24, 30, 37, 38

Ebert, Friedrich 5, 9, 19
economy, German
  1919–23 14, 38
  1929–33 18–19, 20, 32, 38
  1933–45 60–1, 63–6
education 45, 66–7
El Alamein, Battle of (1942) 91, 92
elections to Reichstag 8, 19, 20, 31, 32, 35–6, 38, 40
Enabling Act (1933) 41, 59

Final Solution, the 83–4
Four Year Plan 60–1
France 11, 14, 15, 54, 80
Frank, Anne 86
Freikorps 23, 24
Freisler, Judge Roland 46–7

German Faith Movement 51
German Labour Front (DAF) 49
Gestapo 46, 47, 49, 59, 70, 75
ghettoes 55, 87–8
Goebbels, Joseph 30–1, 37, 38, 44–5, 55, 81–2
Goerdeler, Karl 89
Goering, Hermann 46, 61, 91, 92
Gropius, Walter 16–17

Haeckel, Ernst 27–8
Heidegger, Martin 49
Hess, Rudolf 37, 91
Heydrich, Reinhard 46, 47, 84
Himmler, Heinrich 43, 46, 47, 52, 84
Hindenburg, Paul von 7, 11, 19, 20, 21, 22, 23, 32, 38, 54, 61, 74
Hitler, Adolf 11, 12, 20, 21, 22, 23, 24–6, 32–3, 36, 37, 50–1, 58–9, 60–1, 67, 75–7, 79
  appointed Chancellor 36, 38, 40
  attitude to war 79
  changes strategy 30–1, 37, 38
  death of 91, 92
  early career 24
  economic policies 60–1, 63–6
  becomes Führer 42, 59
  ideas 27–9
  image of 66, 75–7
  imprisonment 26, 30, 37
  and Munich *Putsch* (1923) 12, 22, 24–6
  rise in Nazi Party 24–6
  opposition to 48–51, 89–90
  personal attributes of 37
  and presidential election (1932) 32, 38
  and the racial state 52–5
  rise to power 23–38
Hitler Youth 50, 59, 68–70
Hoess, Rudolf 84, 85–6
Holocaust, the 55, 74, 85–6
Hugenberg, Alfred 35
hyper-inflation 11–12, 22, 25

Jews, persecution of 27–9, 33, 45, 46–7, 53, 83–6

Kahr, Gustav von 23, 25–6
Kaiser 4, 5, 7, 76
Kapp *Putsch* (1920) 12–13, 22, 23, 24
Kellogg-Briand Pact (1928) 15, 22
Kreisau Circle 89
Kristallnacht (1938) 45, 55, 59, 74, 83

Law Against the New Formation of Parties (1933) 41, 42, 59
Law Concerning the Hitler Youth (1936) 50

League of German Maidens 50, 68–9
League of Nations 10, 15, 22
Lebensraum 60
Liebknecht, Karl 5
Lloyd George, David 75
Locarno Pact 15, 22
Lodz, ghetto of 86–7
Lubbe, Marinus van der 41
Luxemburg, Rosa 5

Maidanek 85
Mein Kampf 26–7, 29, 38, 43, 74
middle classes, German 34–5
minority groups, persecution of 47, 74–5
Mother Cross 72
Munich *Putsch* (1923) 12–13, 22, 25–6, 31, 38, 43
Müller, Hermann 9, 19
Mussolini, Benito 25

nationalism 27–8
National Labour Service (RAD) 49, 59
Nazi Party 8, 9, 17, 20, 23, 24–6, 30–1, 32–3, 34–6, 40–1, 43–5, 50–1, 52–3, 63–6, 74–5
Niemoller, Martin 51
Night of the Long Knives (1934) 42–3, 47, 59
Nuremberg Laws (1935) 54, 74
Nuremberg Tribunal 61, 91–2

Olympic Games (1936) 59, 74
opposition to Nazis 48–9, 50–1, 69–70, 89–90

Papen, Franz von 9, 19, 20, 21, 22, 92
People's Court, the 47, 59
Poland 10, 61, 79, 84, 85, 86, 87–8
political parties, German
  Centre Party (Z) 8–9, 19, 21, 31, 35, 36, 40, 41
  Communist Party (KPD) 8–9, 15, 17, 25, 35, 36, 40, 48–9
  Democratic Party (DDP) 8–9, 35, 36
  German Workers' Party (DAP) 8, 23, 24, 27
  Independent Socialist Party (USPD) 8–9
  National Socialist German Workers' Party (NSDAP) see under Nazi Party
  National Party (DNVP) 8–9, 17, 21, 34–5, 36, 40
  People's Party (DVP) 8–9, 15, 31, 35, 36
  Social Democratic Party (SPD) 5, 8–9, 15, 19, 25, 31, 32, 35, 36, 40, 48–9
propaganda 21, 24, 30, 34, 37, 43–5, 49, 59, 71, 72, 80–1
Protestant Church and Nazism 51, 89
Prussia 4, 21, 46, 59, 61

radio 44–5, 76
rearmament 60–1
Red Army 81, 91
Reichstag 6, 7, 19, 23, 31, 32, 38, 40
Reichstag fire (1933) 41, 59
Reichswehr 7, 41
Rentenmark 14
reparations 11, 22
Rhineland, demilitarization of 11
Rhineland, remilitarization of 61
Röhm, Ernst 37, 41–3, 75
Ruhr, occupation of (1923) 12, 22, 25

SA (*Sturm Abteilung*) 24–5, 30, 37, 41–3, 46–7, 53–4, 75
Schacht, Hjalmar 60–1, 92
Scheidemann, Philipp 4, 5, 22
Schleicher, Kurt von 9, 19, 20, 21, 22
Scholl, Hans and Sophie 89
Second Book, Hitler's 27, 29, 79
Social-Darwinism 27–8
socialism 27
Soviet Union 79, 80–1, 84, 85
Spartacist League 5, 22, 24
Speer, Albert 58, 92
SS (*Schutzstaffel*) 46–7, 52, 59
'stab in the back', theory of 13, 21, 29, 33
Stalingrad, Battle of (1942) 91, 92
Stauffenberg, Claus von 89
Strasser, Gregor 30, 31, 38
Streicher, Julius 54, 91
Strength through Joy (KDF) 49, 65
Stresemann, Gustav 8, 14–15, 19, 22, 33
Sudetenland 61

Thyssen, Fritz 35, 37
totalitarianism 20, 43
trade unions 48–9, 65
Treblinka 87
Triumph of the Will 59, 69
Twenty-Five Point Programme 24, 26–7

unemployment 18–19, 29, 63–4
United States of America (USA) 5, 14, 18, 20, 82

Versailles, Treaty of (1919) 10–11, 14–15, 22, 33, 61, 77, 89
Volkswagen, the 66

Wall Street Crash (1929) 18–19, 22, 38
Wannsee Conference (1942) 83
Wehrmacht 42
Weimar Republic
  art and culture in 16–17, 49
  coalitions 7, 9, 15, 38
  Constitution of 6–7, 19, 20, 21, 30, 38, 40–1, 61
  crisis of 1929–33 18–20, 32
  formation of 4–5, 22
  and Stresemann era (1923–9) 14–15, 38
White Rose Movement 89
women, Nazi attitude towards 34, 71–2
World War, First (1914–18) 4, 5, 7, 10, 21, 54, 61
World War, Second (1939–45) 45, 49, 51, 55, 61, 80–2, 83–91

Young Plan (1929) 14, 22